TOPICS IN AUTISM

THIRD EDITION

Siblings of Children with Autism

A GUIDE FOR FAMILIES

Sandra L. Harris, Ph.D. & Beth A. Glasberg, Ph.D., BCBA-D

Sandra L. Harris, Ph.D., series editor

Woodbine House ◆ 2012

Third edition

Published in the United States of America by Woodbine House, Inc.,
6510 Bells Bell Rd., Bethesda, MD 20817. 800-843-7323. www.woodbinehouse.com.

Library of Congress Cataloging-in-Publication Data

Harris, Sandra L.
Siblings of children with autism : a guide for families / Sandra L. Harris and Beth Glasberg. -- 3rd ed.
p. cm. -- (Topics in autism)
Includes index.
ISBN 978-1-60613-074-2
1. Autistic children--Family relationships. I. Glasberg, Beth A. II. Title.
RJ506.A9H27 2012
618.92'85882--dc23

2012003650

Manufactured in the United States of America

10 9 8 7 6 5 4 3 2 1

THIRD EDITION

Siblings of Children with Autism

A GUIDE FOR FAMILIES

For Jay and for Deedee,
who, as our siblings, taught us a great deal about life, love,
and the joys of connection.

Table of Contents

Preface

Between the two of us, we have spent more than half a century serving children, adolescents, and adults with autism spectrum disorders (ASD) and their families. It has been our privilege to get to know many parents, grandparents, brothers, sisters, aunts, and uncles who love a person on the spectrum. Their devotion is often extraordinary. Many of them are people of great patience with a capacity for deep love, and they care intensely about the quality of life of their family member on the spectrum, just as they care about the rest of their family. We have been invited into their homes, shared their joys and sorrows, taken great pride in watching the siblings of their child with an ASD become compassionate and loving adults in their own right, and over the years have joined some of them in mourning the loss of beloved family members. Living in a family that has one or more members who are on the autism spectrum is mostly just like life in any other family, but the complexity of family life is compounded by having to help their family member(s) with an ASD adapt to living in an often bewildering world.

Major advances have been made over the past decade in our ability to understand the ASDs. A variety of genetic links are being discovered, and we now have evidence suggesting that the prenatal environment may be related to some forms of ASD. Using modern imaging equipment including MRIs and CT scans has enabled scientists to look at specific areas of the brain and see how those areas differ in people with ASD from those of neurotypical individuals.

Important advances have also been made in the early identification of infants and toddlers who are at risk for being diagnosed with an ASD by the age of three years. This has created the opportunity to intervene very early in the lives of these children and to begin to learn about the impact our interventions might have on their later development. These exciting advances offer hope that in time we may ultimately be able to target our treatments more precisely and begin intervention at an even earlier age.

While these new findings have the potential to make a great deal of difference in the years ahead, they do not offer much by way of immediate benefits for many of the readers of this book. This means that you need to rely on the best resources that are available today. The research data are consistent in identifying applied behavior analysis (ABA) as having the best empirical evidence to support its use in treating children, adolescents, or adults on the autism spectrum. Fortunately, ABA offers a tool box of procedures that enable behavior analysts, teachers, psychologists, and parents to bring a great many resources to bear on educating the diverse population of people with ASD.

Raising a child with ASD intensifies the demands on a family. Along with the time and financial demands placed on parents, there is also an impact on the brothers and sisters of a child with ASD. This book is aimed at helping you support your children in understanding what ASD is all about and giving your children some simple tools that they can use to form a meaningful relationship with their sibling with ASD.

In private conversations and in parent support groups we have often discussed with mothers and fathers the impact of the child with an ASD on the rest of the family, and especially on the other children in the family. Parents often express concern about their typically developing children and how the time they spend with their child on the spectrum decreases what they have available for the rest of their family. When we meet in sibling support groups with the children and teenagers themselves, we find that most of them have genuine love for their brother or sister on the spectrum and would like to learn how to interact with them more comfortably. They also acknowledge that there are situations when they wish their parents had more time for them, but the older they get, the more they understand why their parents have to spend so much time with their sibling on the spectrum. Younger children are often not clear about what ASD means and teenagers often worry about someday passing along ASD genes to their own children. Teenagers in particular are reluctant to upset their parents by expressing their own fears. We hope the suggestions we offer in this book will give you some ideas about how to have conversations with your preteen or teenager as well as how to help your young child understand ASD at a level appropriate to her developmental level.

If you find the book useful please drop us a line or send us an e-mail to let us know what was helpful to you. We have parents in mind as our primary readers, but grandparents and adult siblings may also find the book useful. Teachers and other professionals have also told us they found the book useful for themselves and as a resource for parents.

This is the third edition of the sibling book. We have done our best to update it to reflect current research and the impact of technology on how people communicate. Computers, smartphones, Twitter, Facebook, and other tools for social communication have provided even parents who live in isolated areas the opportunity to be in touch with other people who share their concerns. We have also described in this book some of the things we have learned clinically since the last edition was published.

We owe heartfelt thanks to the siblings and parents who have talked with us over the years about the realities of their lives. Some of them were families with whom we had direct contact in New Jersey, others were people we met in many places where we were giving talks or consulting, and some we've enjoyed e-mail exchanges with but never met. The parents and adult siblings with whom we talked or corresponded often had helpful suggestions for the next edition of the book or raised questions we had not considered before.

The two of us take full responsibility for the content of this book, but we do want to acknowledge some of the people who have helped us over the years. Nancy Gray Paul, an editor for Woodbine House, has a gift for transforming our professional jargon into user friendly language that conveys our intent without requiring that the reader keep a dictionary at her side! A number of parents, many from the DDDC, but others as well, contributed the comments that you will find at the end of each chapter and/or sent in photographs that you will see throughout the book. We made a few small changes in some of the comments to disguise the identity of the writer, but we have not altered their intent. We thank each of the following families for their contribution to this book: the Carden family, the Cardona family, the Danatos family, the Fogarty family, the Gajewski family, the Gatti family, the Goodwin family, the Larue family, the Locilento family, the McGeehan family, the Shoop family, the Sterling family, and the Zadroga family.

Our colleagues at the Douglass Developmental Disabilities Center including Maria Arnold, Marlene Brown, Lara Delmolino, Kate Fiske Massey, Cat Francis, Barbara Kristoff, Bob LaRue, Donna Sloan, and Kim Sloman were all supportive of our writing this third edition and have been wonderful partners in our collective efforts to improve the lives of people on the autism spectrum. We also thank Jean L. Burton who, as chair of the Douglass College Psychology Department in 1972, supported the creation of the DDDC forty years ago.

Sandra thanks Joseph Masling, her graduate school mentor and now an enduring friend for his unflagging support of her career. She also thanks Han van den Blink for teaching her to appreciate the impact of the family on its individual members and vice versa. Sandra also thanks Rhona Leibel for more than fifty years of friendship from childhood to our current state of "maturity."

Beth thanks Spencer and Tessa, her children, for being such super siblings themselves (most of the time), and Pete, her husband, for always being there for her.

New Brunswick, New Jersey
and
Allentown, New Jersey

1 Brothers and Sisters: Getting to Know You, Getting to Like You, Wondering if You Like Me

The Perez Family

Maria Perez is nine years old with dark hair, deep brown eyes, and a lovely smile. Her younger brother, Roberto, is a handsome, curly haired seven-year-old who goes to Maria's school and has an autism spectrum disorder. From Maria's perspective, that is the biggest problem in her life.

Take yesterday, for example. She was playing soccer with her friends on the playground at recess and having a great time. She had already scored twice and was imagining herself as a famous superstar player. Then, her brother's class came out on the playground and Roberto ran over to Maria right in the middle of the game. He stumbled over the ball, knocking it out of bounds, and gave Maria a big hug. What a humiliation for Maria! She had lost a chance to score, her little brother had messed up the game, and it felt like everyone was mad at her and Roberto. Roberto's teacher, Mr. Max, came over and convinced Roberto to go play in another area of the playground. But the game was already ruined for Maria. She felt ashamed of her brother and embarrassed by what he had done to the game. She began to have dark thoughts about trading Roberto for another brother.

The day before had been even worse. Maria had just finished a math quiz when one of the assistants from Roberto's class came into the room and whispered to Maria's teacher. The teacher called Maria to her desk and the assistant asked if Maria could come with her to help calm Roberto down. He was having a big tantrum. Another humiliation as everyone looked up to see Maria leaving the room. What were the other kids thinking about her? Maybe they thought she had done something wrong. Maybe they thought she was sick. Whatever it was, it couldn't be good.

Life in the same school as Roberto was mishap after another. Maybe tomorrow Maria would tell her mother she felt sick and her mother would let her stay home. The problem was she knew her mother had to go to work and if she stayed home her mother might be mad at her. Besides, if she said she was sick she would have to stay in bed all day and that wasn't any fun. She was trapped!

That night, as her father, Jose, was helping her get ready for bed, Maria began to cry. "I hate school. I don't like going there. People are mean to me." Jose was surprised and concerned to hear the intensity of Maria's distress. As he hugged her he asked very gently what had happened that upset her so much. The words tumbled from her mouth. For weeks she had been enduring all of the problems that Roberto posed at school without complaining to her parents or anyone else. But the burden had gotten to be too much for her. Jose listened quietly while she shared her secret with him. Jose told her he was glad she had told him. He also said he would like to tell her mother about what she had told him, if that was okay. Maria said that was alright and then Jose sat on the edge of the bed for a while and gently sang her a song that his mother used to sing to him when he was a boy in Mexico. Maria drifted off to sleep listening to her father's loving voice.

After Maria fell asleep and Jose's wife, Mia, had gotten Roberto to bed, the parents talked for a while about how to address Maria's problem. They decided they would talk to Maria's teacher and see if she had any suggestions about how to make their daughter's life in school happier than it had been.

Introduction

Living with a child who has an autism spectrum disorder (ASD) has its challenges for every member of the family. Mothers, fathers, grandparents, and siblings are all faced with the difficulties of helping the child with ASD be a part of the family and still managing good lives for themselves. The problems that young Maria Perez is facing are not unusual for children who have a brother or sister with an ASD at the same school. Well-meaning adults may ask the typically developing child to help when his or her sibling with ASD is posing problems. If the child sees her brother or sister being bullied on the playground, the neurotypical sibling (i.e., typically developing) may feel responsible for intervening and end up in the principal's office for fighting. The child

with an ASD may be oblivious to the impact of his behavior on the sibling and interrupt her playing, as Roberto did with Maria.

It is important to know that most siblings and parents work out these problems and can develop plans that respect the needs of the whole family. We will begin this book by summarizing what the research has to tell us about the relationships between brothers and sisters who are developing typically and those whose sibling relationships are influenced by one child's ASD. Chapter 2 examines how a child's understanding of ASD changes as he grows up. In Chapter 3 we look at how a child's developing ability to understand the nature of ASD can guide parents in explaining the disorder to their neurotypical children. Maria Perez had been unable to tell her parents how upset she was about being with her brother at school. Chapter 4 has suggestions for how to improve family communications and facilitate this kind of discussion. One of the challenges that parents face is ensuring that everyone in the family has some private space as well as sharing activities as a family. In Chapter 5, we will consider how the entire family can strike a balance between inclusion and separateness, so that the needs of each family member are met to the extent that's possible. One of the fondest wishes of many young neurotypical children is that their brother or sister with autism will be a playmate. Chapter 6 describes some ways to support play between children when one of them has an ASD. Finally, in Chapter 7 we will consider the needs of the adult sibling.

Every Family is Different

Although many families fit the "classic" picture of a mother, a father, and two children, there are countless variations on this theme. Some families have many more children. Some families are single parent families. Some families have two mothers or two fathers. Some families are headed by a grandmother or grandfather. Some children are raised by their biological parents. Some children are raised by adoptive or step-parents. Some families are deeply embedded in their religious or ethnic traditions; some families are not. Some families have ancestors who have lived in the same country for generations. Some families just arrived in their current country from another nation.

All of these differences in family structure and family values have an impact on how families live their lives. The choices we make, the paths that seem to be the right ones to take, have been, in part, framed by the family culture in which we grew up. We may follow the same path as our parents or take a very different path, but either way, our families have an influence on our choices.

We recognize how much variation there is among families and have tried to be sensitive to these differences in our book. We hope that the ideas we are sharing will be helpful to many different families, regardless of the structure and the values they hold. We also know that different family structures result in different challenges. A single parent family, in many cases, has fewer resources to call upon than a two-parent family. A step-parent who marries someone who has a child with ASD not only has to make an adjustment to that marriage, but also to the realities of raising a child on the autism spectrum. Similarly, a step-child in such a family must not only accept a new step-parent, but also learn how to accommodate a new step-sibling with ASD. Initially, that can feel overwhelming to both the child and the adult who finds himself in a blended family.

Adopting a child also comes with challenges. Some parents know that the child they are adopting has an ASD and want to offer that child a loving family life. Other parents do not discover until some time after the adoption has become final that their child has an ASD diagnosis. Like other parents, they will likely mourn the loss of the child they had expected to raise while doing all they can to help the child they adopted grow up to be as happy and productive as possible. As Brodzinsky and his colleagues (1984) note, adoption can have both a positive and a negative impact on a family.

Some families may find benefit from professional consultations to address the special demands they face. There are a number of professionals to whom you can turn for help in solving problems about a child on the autism spectrum or for concerns about your marriage or family life. Table 1-1 summarizes the roles of these professionals who provide services for people with ASD and their families.

Table 1-1 | Professionals Who May Be Able to Help
Clinical Psychologist—Has a doctorate in psychology and is licensed or certified by state. Clinical psychologists study human behavior and mental processes with the goal of reducing suffering and increasing self-understanding and healthy functioning. May work in public agency or private practice. Does behavioral intervention with child, parent training, diagnosis, and individual, marital, or family therapy. Provides consultation for finding community resources.
Family Therapist—May be a social worker, psychologist, psychiatrist, pastoral counselor, or marriage and family therapist who specializes in work with families.
Neurologist—Has an MD degree with specialized training in brain function. Provides consultation regarding diagnosis, medication, and community resources.
Psychiatrist—Has an MD degree with special training in psychiatry. Because of their medical training, psychiatrists have specialized, in-depth understanding of the biological factors underlying human behavior and have the expertise to prescribe medication and other medical treatments. Provides consultation regarding diagnosis, medication, and community resources. May do individual, marital, or family therapy.
School Psychologist—Has a master's degree or doctorate in school psychology. Licensed or certified by the state. May work in schools, public agencies, or private practice. Provides consultation regarding diagnosis, behavioral intervention for child, parent training, resources in community, and individual, marital, or family therapy.
Special Education Teacher—Has a bachelor's or master's degree in education. Licensed by state. Works in school setting. Provides consultation regarding behavioral intervention with child, parent training, and resources in community.
Board Certified Behavior Analyst—Has passed a national examination in applied behavior analysis (ABA) reflecting a mastery of how to apply the principles of learning to changing human behavior. May come from different helping professions including psychology, speech, and special education. Has received extensive classroom and hands-on supervised training in the use of the techniques of applied behavior analysis. May work in schools, private agencies, or private practice. Provides consultation in the development of teaching programs and behavior management programs for people with autism.

Families and the Genetics of ASD

The siblings of children with an ASD are at greater risk for having an ASD or related symptoms than are other children without a family history of ASD. These siblings are 4 percent to 8 percent more likely to be diagnosed with an ASD than children in the general population. Of course, that low percentage also means that most siblings do not have the genetic vulnerability. However, it was the identification of this genetic vulnerability in a subset of children on the autism spectrum that led researchers to study the baby siblings of older children who were already diagnosed with an ASD. These babies were followed intensively in a search for clues about how ASDs manifest themselves very early in children's development. That research has enabled us to recognize the early indicators that an infant or toddler may be diagnosed with an ASD by three years of age. For example, a study by Rozga (2011) and her colleagues found that during an evaluation at six months of age, baby sibs, who would ultimately develop deficits in social skills, showed no difference from baby sibs who were never given an ASD diagnosis or from low-risk comparison babies in social gaze, affect, or joint attention (following the gaze of another person). However, during evaluations done at twelve months of age, the babies who were eventually diagnosed with ASD showed a lower frequency of joint attention and made fewer requests than those children who were never diagnosed with an ASD.

Not every vulnerable baby sibling shows the full range of symptoms seen in ASD. There is a subgroup of baby sibs who have what researchers call the "broad autism phenotype" (BAP). Toth and her colleagues (2007) studied a group of toddlers who showed these milder (BAP) behaviors. During their early evaluations, nearly 30 percent of the children who exhibited the BAP symptoms had below average IQs, had less mature motor skills, and were lower than their typical peers in their ability to perform daily living skills and respond socially. Fortunately, for many children, these behaviors improved with age and by the time they got to kindergarten they appeared to have largely caught up to their peers (Gamliel, Yirmiya, & Sigman, 2007). Some children did, however, continue to have special needs.

Despite the fact that in some cases of ASD there does appear to be a genetic factor that can express itself in varying degrees from severe symptoms to very mild ones, the occurrence of an ASD diagnosis in more than one child in a family is low, and the very mild BAP behaviors of some siblings may have little to no impact on their lives. In addition, it is unlikely that all people diagnosed with an ASD have a genetic predisposition to the disorder. There is ongoing research exploring other factors that might affect brain function and create behaviors seen in people with an ASD. It is important to remember that there are probably multiple disorders under the broad heading of ASD. A great deal of research remains to be done to help distinguish among these many disorders and the different factors that may be involved in creating at least a superficial similarity among children who may actually have various forms of ASD.

For parents who have two or more children with an ASD, or one child with an ASD and another who continues to exhibit symptoms of the BAP beyond early childhood, life can be very complex. We know several families who have to not only ensure that their child with ASD gets essential services, but also need to ensure appropriate services for their child with milder symptoms. These families may need a great deal of social support.

Siblings across a Lifetime

Brothers and sisters have a unique relationship and one that doesn't end when childhood does. These relationships, at least in their formal sense, continue across our lifetime. For many adults, the person who has known us the longest and best is our sibling. However, the quality of sibling relationships varies widely, and some of us are blessed with a sense of intimacy in our interactions with our brother or sister, while others of us hardly know this person with whom we share a profound biological bond. Although we choose our friendships,

our brothers and sisters are imposed on us, and even if we are emotionally or geographically distanced from them, they remain part of the fabric of our lives.

In thinking about how your children get along with each other, it is helpful to understand that there are a variety of types of sibling relationships that are "normal." You should also know that sibling relationships change as children grow up. There is no single prescription for how brothers and sister should get along.

The Sibling Bond

During childhood, siblings spend many hours together, and based on that continuing interaction, develop their own relationship, which is often very close and protective. The concept of the "sibling bond" was described more than a quarter century ago when psychologists Stephen Bank and Michael Kahn (1982) interviewed several hundred siblings of different ages, gender, and social backgrounds. They found that ease of access is one of the factors that support the development of a tight emotional connection between siblings. A strong sibling bond is most liable to grow when children are relatively close in age, are of the same gender, and have done many things together. The converse, a weaker bond, is more likely to arise when children are born far apart, are of different genders, and have done relatively few things together. Bank and Kahn note that a strong bond is not always a positive bond. While many siblings with a strong bond derive considerable pleasure from each other's company, there are some for whom the bond is filled with tension and negative feelings.

Early Childhood

To understand the relationship between a neurotypical child and his sibling with autism it helps to know something about how typically developing children come to love one another. Sibling relationships evolve over time. Feelings about each other change from the age of five years, to fifteen years, to thirty-five years, to fifty-five years. As we mature and change, so do our relationships with our brothers or sisters. When we think about young children, our thoughts may turn to the notion of sibling rivalry and the feelings of the older children when a baby is born. Parents will often say that they can't imagine loving another child as much as they do their firstborn, but when the new baby arrives, she immediately becomes just as precious as the older child. The older child may have a very different view! Along with some curiosity, he may feel impatient for this new baby to go away so he can return to being the center of his parents' universe.

Learning to love the interloper in his life takes time. Your older child may temporarily regress in some of his toileting skills, become withdrawn, aggressive, or anxious after a new baby enters the family (Cicirelli, 1995). These behaviors are usually transient, and the older child gradually learns to share his parents with the new arrival. This happens best when parents take an active role in supporting the older child as he comes to terms with the changes in his life. Adults may expect the older child to rejoice in the baby just as they have. But for the older child, it is often a dramatic and possibly unwanted change in his life. Lots of love and reassurance as well as clear rules are in order for the older child as he makes the transition into his new role.

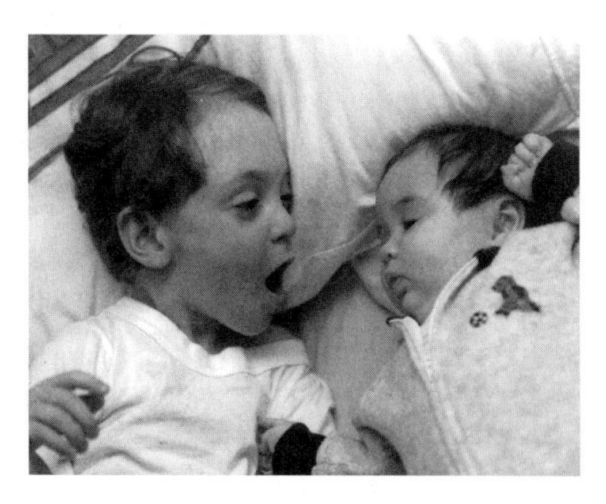

Building the Relationship

As the newborn becomes responsive to the smiles of her sibling and smiles back at him, and as they start to be able to interact, the older child begins to take an interest in the baby. He can be a model of how to do things, can teach his sibling new skills, can comfort the younger child, and become the leader of the games they play (Cicirelli, 1995). When the younger child is between three and four years of age she has enough skills to be a good companion for childhood play. The important skills include more complex motor skills, language, and a broad array of social responses. These developmental changes increase the interest of the older child in the younger, and make it likely that they will spend more time together (Dunn, 1992). This extended time together does, however, cut both ways, increasing both their level of companionship and their feelings of competition with one another. Buhrmester (1992) notes that children who are close in age will have more quarrels and more tension in their relationships than will children who are separated by four or more years, but that they will also have a closer emotional bond than children with a greater age difference.

It is not surprising that those parents who have a good relationship with one another and who can resolve differences of opinion without resorting to arguing are likely to have children who use that model to relate well to one another and resolve their differences. Mothers and fathers who are effective in their parenting role are likely to raise children who have good relationships with one another (Boer, Goedhart, & Treffers, 1992). As shown in Table 1-2, these parents make a point to convey their respect, warmth, and love to their children. They also have clear and consistent expectations and standards for their children's behavior and set limits on inappropriate behaviors. In addition, these parents are likely to provide predictable but flexible routines for their children.

Table 1-2 | Helpful Parenting Behaviors
1. Convey respect, warmth, and love.
2. Remain consistent in expectations and rules.
3. Set clear limits on inappropriate behaviors.
4. Provide predictable but flexible childhood routines.

Middle Childhood and Adolescence

Dunn (1992) identified a major change in the sibling relationship during middle childhood. She found a shift that results in greater equality, with the younger child needing less caretaking by the age of eleven or twelve years of age, and the older child beginning to move into the wider social world of adolescence. The older child, who initially dominated the interactions with the younger child, now makes room for a more equal balance in power so that both youngsters share control over their relationship and activities. Buhrmester (1992) notes that greater equality between the children allows more independence for the younger sibling and opens the door for the older sibling to pursue adolescent goals. Slomkowski and Manke (2004) summarize the research on sibling relationships during these years by writing that warmth

and conflict both diminish during late middle childhood and early adolescence. Interestingly, they also report that unlike the other age/gender combinations, two sisters are likely to show an increase in warmth and self-disclosure during this period.

Adulthood

Sibling relationships endure for our lifetime. After many years spent pursuing their own lives in regard to marriage, work, and other activities, many adult siblings interact more than they had for some decades. Friendships may be lost in moves, marriages dissolve, and parents die, but the sibling relationship typically endures through all of these transitions. In our later years, our brother or sister may remain the sole link to our past.

When a Brother or Sister Has Autism

The sibling relationship in a family where one child has an ASD and the other is neurotypical (i.e., typically developing) creates a different experience than the normative sibling bond. A young girl who wants to play dolls with her younger sister will be deeply disappointed if her sister's only response is to toss the doll or scream when her sister approaches her. Even the most persistent of children is likely to give up trying to engage a brother or sister who either passively or actively refuses to join in play. Rather than building connections, these efforts at childhood play are often very punishing for the neurotypical child who feels ineffectual in trying to engage with her sibling who has ASD. Her sadness and frustration may result in her seeking playmates in other contexts and largely ignoring her sister on the spectrum. That does not mean she no longer feels sad about the loss of a potential playmate, but rather that she no longer expects she can form that kind of connection. The fondest wish of many young neurotypical children is that they could play with their sibling on the autism spectrum. How painful it is to fail in that attempt.

A school-aged child will be understandably angry if his brother on the spectrum comes into his room and tosses a prized possession on the floor where it shatters into many pieces. Children of any age may feel excluded and ignored when the major focus of parental attention is on the child with an ASD. In many cases, the more marginalized they feel, the harder it becomes for them to voice their concerns to their parents. In the description of Maria Perez and her brother Roberto that opened this chapter we saw how hard it was for her to bring her concerns to her parents. She did not want to upset them and she did not want to make them angry. She was ashamed of her "bad thoughts."

Feelings of resentment and jealousy are not unique to families in which there is a child with ASD. Birth order can contribute to a sense of inequality that often creates feelings of frustration and competition in any family. "How come he can stay up later than me?" "How come he can go to the store by himself?" "Why do you do so many things for her and tell me I have to do it for myself?" "Why do I have to take out the trash if she doesn't?" Whether we are the oldest, youngest, or some place in the middle, opportunities vary by age and can stir resentment in the child who is not receiving the same benefits. It is important to recognize that these feelings can be a part of a normative level of childhood competition as contrasted with a much more substantial feeling of loss experienced by some siblings of children on the autism spectrum.

It is reassuring to know that most children who have a sibling with ASD learn to handle their feelings of sadness, loss, and anger and are as psychologically healthy as their peers on many measures of emotional functioning (e.g., Grissom & Borkowski, 2002). Rodrigue, Geffken, and Morgan (1993) found that while the brothers and sisters of children with autism reported more feelings of sadness and worry as well as more acting out behavior than did siblings of children with Down syndrome, or siblings with a neurotypical brother or sister, the average scores for psychological well-being of the ASD sibling group fell within the normative (i.e., typical) range and did not reflect psychopathology. Also on the positive side, they found that the siblings of children with autism did not differ from the two comparison groups in terms of self-esteem. However, normative psychological functioning does not diminish the

reality that growing up with a sibling who has an ASD poses an enduring challenge to the neurotypical sibling. Some children learn to deal with the challenges with relative grace while others have much more difficulty coping effectively with the demands they encounter. If parents are attuned to the challenges that face their children they may be able to respond proactively by talking about the child's feelings and possible solutions to the problems they encounter. If you can help your neurotypical child feel better, you too are likely to feel better.

Susan McHale and her colleagues (1986), in a study of children between six and fifteen years of age, found that these youngsters had mostly positive things to say about their sibling regardless of whether the sibling had autism, mental retardation (now called intellectual disability), or were developing typically. They do, however, note that while some siblings had mostly positive things to say, there were others who gave more negative descriptions. The children who gave negative reports often said they were concerned about the future of the child with a disability, and held the belief that their parents favored that child. In contrast, the children who viewed both parents and peers as responding positively to the child's disability and who had a good factual understanding of the disability tended to have a more positive relationship with their brother or sister. A major focus of this book is aimed at how you can provide your neurotypical child with the knowledge and experience to hold a positive view of his relationship with his sibling with ASD.

The sibling research is consistent with our own clinical experiences. Most of the siblings we know are resilient in the face of the special needs of their brother or sister with ASD. But, as noted above, there are challenges involved in growing up with a brother or sister who has an ASD and it is important that neurotypical siblings receive the support they need to meet these challenges.

Special Demands

The Need for Information

One of us (BG) has studied in depth the information needs of neurotypical siblings at different ages. Providing children with age appropriate information is one of the important things that parents can do to help their neurotypical child cope. A lack of information leaves a big space in the child's mind to be filled by misinformation, fears, and fantasies. Children will create their own explanations, worry needlessly about whether they harmed their sibling, or imagine a future life for themselves or their sibling far bleaker than reality.

Young children in particular have a difficult time distinguishing wish from reality, and may become very confused about their sibling's disability. Although they hear the word "autism," they may not understand what it means. They may, for example, be afraid that they caused the ASD by some misbehavior or angry thought, or that they can "catch" ASD as they would a cold. To compound matters, as noted earlier in the case of Maria Perez, children might be afraid to raise problems because they do not wish to upset their parents or because they are ashamed of their own feelings or anger, jealousy, or resentment. The research by BG suggests that some children have problems communicating their concerns and may feel overly responsible for the welfare of their sibling with ASD. Children growing up under these conditions may learn to conceal feelings, deny their emotions to themselves, and develop an inconsistency between feelings and actions. For example, a child might be frightened, but rather than expressing fear, he might act very boldly in a way that could place him in danger, or he might act as though he wanted no support or affection, when he actually wishes that his parents would recognize his sadness. These behaviors can intrude on their capacity as adults for intimacy and form a barrier to relationships with other people. Fortunately, it is usually possible for parents to recognize and address these childhood concerns.

Having difficulties understanding about ASD can also diminish a child's feeling of being a unique and special person, entitled to lead a separate life. Some children may overly identify with their sibling and feel responsible for his disability (Seligman and Darling, 1977). A lack of information may make it difficult for the typically developing child to have a clear sense of himself as a unique person, not an extension of his brother. For example, a boy may be reluctant to go away to summer camp because his younger brother with ASD cannot go as well. It may be hard for him to understand that he can have a separate, happy life apart from his brother. Over time, if he continues to have trouble separating himself from his brother, he may grow up to be an adult who cannot lay claim to the basic right to exist as a special, unique person. In order to establish healthy adult relationships, we need to experience the legitimacy of our own needs as well as others' needs. Again, a perceptive parent can often recognize the seeds of such a problem.

In Chapter 2 we will discuss in depth what children think and feel about ASD and the potential impact it will have on them and their siblings in the years that lie ahead. Chapter 3 will help you target your information about ASD to the age of your child and the issues that are likely to be most salient at that developmental stage. This information may give your child a realistic sense of his sibling's special needs and why there are differences in how the two of them are treated.

Play Skills

Play is one of the most important activities of childhood. It is not only pleasurable, but allows children to practice roles, develop new skills, share decision making with a playmate, and rehearse anticipated events. Siblings of children with ASD long for a playful relationship with their brother or sister. In Chapter 6 we will explain how to teach your neurotypical child how to engage his brother or sister in play that is appropriate to the skills of the child with ASD. There is good research showing that children can learn these simple skills and apply them when they play with their sibling on the spectrum. This shared experience has the potential to strengthen the sibling bond and give the neurotypical child a sense of empowerment.

Caretaking Responsibilities

In families with typically developing children it is common for older children, especially girls, to take some responsibility for their younger brother or sister. In these families, as the younger siblings reach early adolescence, this responsibility usually decreases because the younger child is now capable of much more independent functioning. The situation is different in families where there is an older neurotypical child and a younger child with ASD. In this scenario, older neurotypical sisters are likely to be asked to assume a caretaker role and some brothers also assume this role, although not as often as girls (McHale & V. Harris, 1992). For example, an older sister may help her brother with autism dress in the morning or supervise his play while parents prepare dinner. Because the child on the spectrum often is not able to care for himself even as he gets older, the sibling's caretaking role continues over time. When the older child is ready to leave home to go to college, join the military, or take a job, it can create a crisis for the family when one of the primary sources of parental support is withdrawn. Alternatively, some older siblings may feel an obligation to remain at home to care for their brother or sister on the spectrum. Parents need to be alert to the danger of allowing their older child to be so devoted a caretaker that it interferes with that youngster's social development and ability to have an independent life.

The inequities of the caretaking relationship can affect younger siblings as well as older ones. When the firstborn child has an ASD and the second child is neurotypical, a reversal of the usual caretaking roles is created in that the younger may become the caretaker for the older. For example, a nine-year-old sister may find herself looking after a thirteen-year-old brother, in stark contrast to the typical age-appropriate roles she sees in other families. She may resent or even be fearful of having to care for someone who is physically older and larger, or be embarrassed to have her friends see her caring for him. She may also feel guilty about being younger but more competent than her big brother. In the normal course of events, older children care for younger ones, and children may be acutely aware of being different from their peers in this regard. The sense of being different can make a child feel angry, ashamed, sad, embarrassed, or defiant. She many avoid being with her brother, not want to have friends over to play when he is home, or perhaps join in when her friends tease him.

Children, older or younger, should not be expected to be auxiliary parents to their sibling on the spectrum. The time demands should be reasonable and if a child with ASD poses significant behavior problems his sibling should never be expected to care for him beyond summoning a parent if the child with ASD is getting out of control.

Everyone who reads this book knows how it feels to be angry. It is a common human emotion. The siblings of a child with ASD are not exempt from that feeling. Maria Perez felt angry about how Roberto intruded on her soccer game and having to leave her classroom to help his teacher calm him down. A child who has to spend most of his after school hours caring for his brother with ASD, who is reluctant to bring friends home because his brother strips off his clothing, and feels that he is always the loser in the competition for parental attention is likely to feel marginalized and experience a great deal of anger as well as sadness.

Contributing to the family by doing some caretaking for a sibling on the spectrum need not be harmful to a child. In Chapter 5 we describe how balancing the needs of every family member is an essential and delicate art. One of these challenges is to assign roles to children that are age and physical size appropriate. Chapter 5 focuses on communication within the family.

Celebrate the Good Times

Although much of this book is focused on resolving problematic family dynamics, there can be, of course, plenty of joy in a household that includes a child with a developmental disability. Your other children can join you in taking pride in the things their brother on the spectrum accomplishes. If he competes in the Special Olympics, learns to speak, can ride a bike and keep up the other kids, or learns how to play coopera-

tively, those are all achievements that merit moments of delight. The siblings should, of course, also have many opportunities to celebrate their own successes. Learning to ice skate, mastering karate moves, playing the piano, getting good grades in school, showing kindness to another child are all times to celebrate. So too are the achievements of mothers and fathers.

Adults will often say that their experience as a sibling of a child with a disability, whether autism, intellectual disability, or a mobility disorder, taught them a patience and tolerance they might not otherwise have learned. In fact, they tend to go into the helping professions in greater numbers than do adults who grew up with a neurotypical sibling. We will discuss this in more depth in Chapter 7 when we look at the experiences of adult siblings.

Adulthood

Earlier in this chapter we wrote about the enduring nature of the sibling relationship. Those siblings who were close as children are likely to remain close as adults, although in early adulthood, when they are busy establishing their own lives, they may share less than they will when they get older. Under the best of conditions, neurotypical siblings have an intimate relationship that is a source of support for their entire lives.

The relationship between a neurotypical adult and his adult sibling with ASD is more complex than that of two neurotypical adults. As long as parents are relatively young and healthy, the sibling may have very few responsibilities for the adult with ASD. But, as parents age and ultimately die, the sibling almost always finds himself drawn into a larger role with his sibling. In some cases that might mean taking him to live in his home, in others it might mean visiting him regularly in a group home or supervised apartment, or in some cases in which the sibling with ASD has achieved a great deal of independence, including living on his own and working, it may mean keeping a watchful eye on his brother in case problems arise.

These responsibilities may not be excessive or burdensome, and are often viewed as an act of love from one sibling to another. However, the continuing requirements of a brother or sister with ASD can pose significant additional demands when combined with the adult sibling's needs to care for his own children, his aging parents, his marriage, and work responsibilities. In addition, adults who have siblings with an ASD have shared their sense of sadness when they could not seek solace from their sibling after a painful event such as the death of a parent. Instead, they had to bear the burden of their sorrow alone, take on all of the administrative responsibilities of the estate, and respond to the ongoing needs of their sibling as well.

For some neurotypical siblings who failed to come to terms with their brother or sister with autism in childhood, adulthood offers new opportunities, as well as new demands. Some people may enter adulthood without having understood the full range of their feelings toward their sibling with autism, or without having come to terms with these emotions. They may enter adulthood with very little sense of connection to their brother or sister with ASD. The feelings of anger, jealousy, resentment, and sense of loss may linger and influence their behavior in adulthood.

One of the good things about being an adult is having the opportunity to establish a new and different relationship with one's sibling on the spectrum. One woman we know entered therapy as an adult because she could not get beyond the anger she felt whenever her brother visited her. She was typically a gentle and compassionate person who was very much admired by her friends, but she could not grow beyond her childhood feelings for her brother. A short course of therapy helped her work out some of the old feelings she held toward her brother and her parents. She realized her anger had less to do with her brother's current behavior than with the expectations she had carried from her childhood. Eventually she was able to set those feelings aside so she could relate to her family with the same respect and caring she brought to other relationships.

Closing Comments

We have briefly looked at sibling relationships, noting that some anger, jealousy, and competition is part of every sibling relationship. Although sibling relationships change as we grow up, many people are fortunate enough to have a caring connection with their sibling throughout their entire lives. For the sibling of a child with an ASD, creating that kind of enduring bond is more difficult. Children with an ASD are less likely to be nurturing, playful, or engaged with their brother or sister than are neurotypical children. They also usually require more caretaking than do typically developing children and do not follow the normative path to increasing independence. Although most children learn to cope with the needs of their sister or brother with an ASD, there is an important role for parents in facilitating this understanding and helping the neurotypical child learn the essential skills to build that relationship. The rest of this book is devoted to helping you—the parents—master these skills so that you can teach them to your child.

Parents Speak

This evening was particularly painful for us. We moved our dinner location from our kitchen table to the dining room, in hopes that the hum of the refrigerator is the thing that sets Juan off each night. We have had other suspicions for a while now. This evening's dinner started on a more challenging note than usual. Juan began to cry and screech from the moment we sat down. We said, "Juan, you need to sit quiet so we can eat." We provided him with the things he generally wants but cannot yet request verbally. Nothing worked.

Suddenly Juan's brother, Manuel, spoke up. "It's me, Dad. Every time he looks at me he cries." I couldn't bring myself to agree with him, but I know it's true. There are no words sufficient to explain how this breaks our hearts. There is no reason for Juan to be upset by his brother. His brother is a wonderful child. He has the gift of unwavering patience and love for his brother Juan. Far more than any nine-year-old I have ever met. He has been bitten and scratched and screamed at, yet he still tries to play with his brother. We must do something to identify the source of Juan's frustration.

My wife said to Manuel, "That's funny. Maybe it is you." As if we didn't already know. "Would you mind finishing dinner in the other room so we can see if Juan will calm down?" she asked. "Sure, Mom," said Manuel. Immediately, there was peace at the dinner table. How do we make this OK for Manuel? How do we mend his heart?

Having a sibling with autism has been very different for Sam and Martha. To some degree, I think the birth order and personality of siblings has an impact on what the relationship will be like. For example, Sam, being the older brother, has always seen Tommy as the baby. He has been understanding of Tom's needs, including all the extra time we have needed to spend with him. When Sam was younger he would get angry at Tom for touching his toys or messing up his room. As he has matured, he has shown compassion beyond his years. At times I think it has made him a kinder, gentler person.

Martha has had a more difficult time adjusting to Tommy. She is four years younger and he seemed to strike out at her more often. She experienced many problems dealing with him and it took time to get to the point where we are now. She has a great love for him but at the same time a fear of him. Even though she knows he is older, she thinks of him as her younger sibling.

Tommy has had a profound effect on his siblings and, like it or not, will probably to some extent shape who they are as adults.

Stan is seven and has autism. His older sister, Sally, is nine. I worry a lot about what it means to grow up with a little brother like Stan. I want her to be able to bring her friends home and I don't want her to be afraid of him. I know our home has to be a little different than other homes, and I don't know how that will affect her emotionally as she grows up.

I think the thing that worries me most about Art is how he is going to feel about Jack as they grow up together. Here is Art, a little guy at age five, telling his big brother Jack, who is eleven, how to do things. I mean, what he is going to think about that as he gets older? Big brothers are supposed to take care of little guys, not the other way around. I'm concerned that it must be confusing to Art.

Justin is such a terrific kid. Sometimes I think he is almost too good. He spends so much time with his sister, Allie, who has autism. He acts like it is his job to do everything for her. I don't want him to resent that someday—to feel like she stole his childhood. I appreciate his help, but I don't want him to overdo. I'm not sure how much help is too much.

2 What Are They Thinking?! Autism Viewed through Children's Eyes

As soon as the show ended, thirteen-year-old Braden pushed past his parents, past his buddies, and bee-lined his way to the family car. His mother, Louisa, and his father, Jim, looked at each other, dumbfounded, and decided to divide and conquer. Louisa agreed to wait for their twelve-year-old daughter, Kaylee, until she was finished backstage, while Jim went to check on Braden. Luckily, they had been able to get a babysitter for Kyle, their ten-year-old son with autism. Otherwise, Jim was sure he would never have made it this far in the evening without a family drama. He was thrilled to have been able to allow Kaylee her special night. She had a starring role in her middle school's production of the play, "Tommy," and she had done a wonderful job.

Jim met Braden at the car. "What's going on?" he asked his son. Braden didn't respond. "I can't help you if I don't know what is going on, and I want to help. Come on, give me a chance to help."

Braden looked unsure, but then spoke, "It's about the show, and it's about Kyle."

"What is it?" Jim asked.

"Well, in the show, I saw how Tommy witnessed these horrible crimes and he was told, 'You didn't see anything, and you didn't hear anything....'"

"What does that have to do with Kyle?" Jim pressed.

"Well, Tommy couldn't talk because of that, and Kyle can't talk, so I got to wondering.... Do you think he saw something horrible? Do you think something horrible happened to him?"

Jim was stunned. He and his wife had spoken openly with Braden and Kaylee about their brother's ASD and the biological and medical nature of the disorder. Why was Braden now presenting him with some voodoo-ish theory? He couldn't understand how they had gotten to this point after all of the information that they had shared. He shuddered to think what else Braden might be thinking about his brother's disability.

Successful communication involves two parts: 1) A speaker shares information, and 2) a listener understands the information that was shared. Without both sides of this equation, communication cannot occur. For example, I do not speak Japanese. If someone tells me that I am driving the wrong way on a one-way street in Japanese, I will likely continue to drive the same way I had been going. Since I did not understand the speaker, no communication has occurred.

Similarly, if someone speaks to a typically developing sibling about ASD in a way that she does not understand, she will not gain any information. Because of the abstract and confusing nature of ASDs, this act of "sharing" can be a challenge. Parents are forced to figure out how much information to share (if any), what specifically needs to be said, how to best say what needs to be said, as well as when and where to have the conversation. All of these decisions can be overwhelming for parents, who probably know very few people who have been through all of this to go to for advice.

Many adults choose not to share information about autism with their neurotypical child because they feel it is too difficult for her to comprehend—only to later discover that she already got the information from another source and understands the matter perfectly. Other adults may choose to share a great deal of information with a child about autism only to discover that what their child heard resembles the droning sound of the adult voice on the old Charlie Brown cartoons! Most often, what children grasp of our explanations probably falls somewhere in between these two extremes: they have heard something that we have said, and have reshaped it somewhat. Unfortunately, the concept that was formed may only faintly resemble the information that we thought we shared.

Once a parent has decided to open the lines of communication about ASD, it may be a challenge to figure out exactly how to get started. Finding the right moment and the right words are not always easy, especially when trying to share complex information with a child whose abilities to comprehend are ever changing. For example, a mom will have to speak very differently to her five-year-old child than she will to her eighteen-year-old young adult child. As much as we want to keep their questions and concerns tied up in neat little packages, those pesky children insist on growing and evolving! It can be difficult for a caregiver to find the right words to explain autism and its effects on family life.

If the information that a parent shares is not a match for what the child can understand, a misunderstanding may result. The adult thinks that certain information was communicated, while the child has not learned anything or may be, in fact, more confused than before. One possible culprit for this type of communication breakdown is a process called "cognitive development." This term refers to changes in our ability to think and acquire knowledge as we mature.

As the famous developmental psychologist Jean Piaget (1929) taught us, children filter information through a developmental lens. This lens limits the level of abstract and complex information that they can process based on their cognitive development. It also alters the importance of different types of information for them. What matters to us as adults may hold little interest for a child. Because parents and professionals may not understand how a child's developmental level affects her understanding, there is a risk that siblings may either miss facts or misconstrue them when we offer them information about autism.

This type of communication breakdown was demonstrated during a research project completed by one of the authors (BG), where siblings ranging in age from five to seventeen years were interviewed about autism and how it affected their lives. Parents were also interviewed and asked to predict how their children would respond. The first question was simply whether or not the sibling had heard the word "autism" (or whichever ASD label the parents indicated had been used in the home, such as Asperger's or PDD). While almost 100 percent of the parents thought that their typically developing child would be familiar with their brother or sister's diagnostic label, almost 20 percent of the children insisted that they had never heard that term before. After the interviews, participating parents had the opportunity to listen to the recorded interviews with their typically developing children. The parents of the children who had claimed they had not known the word were generally very surprised and indicated that they had shared information about the diagnosis with the child. It is likely that the parents had, in fact, shared the information, but because it was not shared in a way that was a match for their child's developmental level, the circuit of communication was not complete.

Another possible explanation for the typically developing children who did not recognize their brother or sister's diagnostic label, despite having discussed it with parents, was that the conversations took place at a specific time and ended at that specific time. The topic may not have resurfaced again. For example, some parents explained that they had sat the typically developing child down when they received the ASD diagnosis and described it...but then never discussed it again. It was not presented as an ongoing discussion. While this may breed some familiarity with the topic, it teaches the child not to raise questions or concerns. It sends the message that the topic is "a big deal," and is not discussed informally. This is similar to what many parents may have heard about teaching children about sexuality. While sitting kids down and having "the talk" may be better than not sharing information at all, it is far more effective to establish an open door policy about sexuality related topics, in which parents themselves raise the topics on their own to model for their children that it is okay to ask questions and express concerns.

How Do Children Develop an Understanding of Illness?

With regard to children's understanding of illness, enough research has been completed to give us a framework for seeing the very specific developmental stages of comprehension. Roger Bibace and Mary Walsh (1979, 1980) devised a method of interviewing children and coding responses so that the *structure* of the response or way of thinking about the illness (cognitive developmental level) could be distinguished from the *content* of the response (fact, belief, or misinformation about the illness). They asked children twelve questions

about illness-related concepts such as health, colds, heart attacks, and germs (Bibace & Walsh, 1979). For each concept, questions focused on what the illness was and how one developed it. Initial answers were followed by open-ended probes such as, "Tell me more" or "Anything else?" This continued until the child had no new information to contribute. Based on these interviews, the authors identified various stages and sub-stages in the developmental progression toward full adult comprehension of health and illness.

Their research revealed that between two and six years of age, children rely on whatever they have seen or heard, more than they rely on parental explanations or logic. Think of the typically developing toddler who would like to eat a lollipop that she found on the ground, or the kindergartner who knows that medicine will make her earache go away but still refuses to take it because she remembers that it tastes bad. For a child this age, first-hand experience guides decision making. Specific to illness, these young children progress through three general phases of reasoning:

1. "**Incomprehension**"—where the child's answers to questions are nonsensical or she does not answer. (For example: "The flu is like French fries. I love French fries! I eat them with ketchup. My mommy doesn't like ketchup....")
2. "**Phenomenism**"—where the child focuses on one specific, concrete symptom or manifestation of the illness. (For example: "The flu is when your Mommy stays in her bedroom and you have to stay outside and let her sleep.")

3. "**Contagion**"—where the child views illness and cure as almost magically transmitted from objects near a person. (For example: "The flu is what you get when you play with somebody who was just sick.")

Next, during middle childhood, from approximately seven through ten years of age, children still maintain their focus on observable events, but their reasoning becomes less limited to personal experience and more logical. In other words, they try to make sense of things. Children in this age group typically progress through two levels of reasoning about illness:

1. "**Contamination**"—indicated by a belief that bad behavior or thoughts, in addition to germs, can lead to illness. Also, multiple symptoms are now considered at one time. (For example: "The flu is when you sneeze, feel achy, and get very sleepy. You can get it when you play out in the cold and forget to put your hat on like your dad told you to.")
2. "**Internalization**"—indicated by a belief that illnesses and cures come from inside the body, rather than outside of it. The child now focuses on the fact that the illness must somehow enter your body in order to make you sick. (For example: "You get the flu when somebody sneezes on your food and their germs land in your plate and you eat them.") A very young child might understand that if you are close to somebody with an illness, you can catch it—but they wouldn't really have an explanation of how that happens. In contrast, a child in this stage would focus on the fact that the illness had to get inside of the person somehow in order to make her ill.

Finally, about eleven years of age and older, children begin to think more like adults. They can now consider possible scenarios and use knowledge rather than immediate perception to reason. Within this stage of development, there are two sub-stages of reasoning:

1. "**Physiological**"—where illness is seen as due to a malfunctioning or nonfunctioning body part, and the individual becomes aware of gaps in her knowledge. (For example: "During the flu, germs attack the lining of your nose, throat, and chest causing them to produce

too much mucus. I'm not sure how the germs cause your body to do that, though.")

2. "**Psycho-physiological**"—where the individual recognizes the influence of the mind on the body. (For example: "I probably caught the flu because my resistance was down from dealing with so much stress lately.")

While these stages and corresponding ages have been demonstrated to accurately depict the developing understanding of illness for most children, interestingly, these findings have not held up for siblings of individuals with these illnesses. For example, Carandang et al. (1979) studied siblings of children with diabetes and found that the siblings actually reasoned about their brother or sister's illness at a less mature level than would be predicted based on norms. This contrasts with the research summary presented by Poltorak & Glazer (2006) regarding children with cancer, which suggests that children who actually experience this illness reason about the illness in a relatively mature fashion. This may be a difference attributable to features of the respective illnesses, or it might be related to the contrast between being a patient and being the sibling of a patient.

Siblings' Understanding of Autism: The Glasberg Study

While researchers have examined how children think about various abstract concepts at different ages, such as death (Poltorak & Glazer, 2006), adoption (Brodzinsky et al., 1984), or divorce (Kurdek, 1986), and researchers have examined how typically developing children think about various illnesses such as cancer (Knighting et al, 2011), or AIDS (Osborne, Kistner, & Helgemo, 1993), a surprisingly scant amount of research has been done

examining how children think about autism at different ages (Glasberg, 2000). However, the existing research on children's understanding of illness suggests how siblings of children with autism may conceptualize autism. From research in other areas, we know that children tend to understand these difficult concepts in an increasingly complex and sophisticated manner with age, and we know that children tend to make jumps in their understanding at certain ages, and therefore we can think about their understanding as developing in stages.

Because autism is a developmental disability rather than an illness, and is associated with less tangible physical symptoms than the flu or cold, we need to determine to what extent the established developmental stages (Bibace & Walsh, 1979, 1980) apply to children's knowledge of autism. In order to confirm that we can expect these same patterns, one of the authors (BG) used a modified version of Bibace and Walsh's interview method with sixty-three siblings aged five to seventeen from New York, New Jersey, and Pennsylvania. In addition to being asked about various concepts of ASD, the siblings were asked about the impact of ASD on themselves and their affected siblings (see Table 2-1). Furthermore, parents were interviewed and asked to predict their children's responses to these questions. This was done in order to help us understand not only what the children understood, but also how well their parents understood their children's reasoning style. At the end of each meeting, parents had the option to listen to their child's recorded interview.

As in the work of Bibace and Walsh (1979), questions initially focused on what autism is and how one gets it. Open-ended probes con-

Table 2-1 | Questions for Siblings

- Have you ever heard of the word "autism"? Tell me about it.
- How do people get autism?
- You've told me a lot about autism. How does having autism make your sister's life different than it would be without autism?
- When she grows up, how will autism make your sister's life different than it would have been without autism?
- How does having a sister with autism make your life different than it would have been if she did not have autism?
- When you grow up, will having a sister with autism make your life different than if you had a sister without autism?

tinued until a child had no new information to add. In addition, certain content areas were specifically addressed with follow-up questions if the child did not spontaneously raise a given topic. For example, if a child did not mention the effect of autism on behavior or the possibility of catching autism, she was asked about these ideas. Finally, as noted above, these children were asked about the ways that ASD has affected their lives as well as the lives of their siblings with autism.

What Did Siblings in the Study Say About ASD?

Although the primary focus of this study was to assess *how* children think about autism at different stages rather than *what* they think about autism at different stages, a brief examination of the content of their responses confirmed our suspicions that what parents share and what children grasp from the interaction may be quite different. The children we talked to often demonstrated either a lack of information or misinformation about autism. For example, approximately one out of every five children claimed that they had never heard the word "autism." This included almost half of the five- through six-year-olds, about a fifth of seven- through ten-year-olds, and one of the eleven- through seventeen-year-olds. Because almost every one of the parents had predicted that their child would be familiar with this word, it is likely that the term had been mentioned by parents and either forgotten by the child or not understood.

Similarly, siblings demonstrated a surprising amount of misinformation. Approximately a quarter of the children either thought that autism could be contagious, or were not sure whether or not it could be contagious. While almost all of the children in the oldest age group were aware that autism could not be "caught," only about half of the seven- through ten-year-olds and two-thirds of the five-through six-year-olds shared this knowledge. A question then arises as to whether these children believe that they might catch autism from their sibling. The following excerpt from an interview with an eight-year-old boy exemplifies the reasoning that children might use to explain why they haven't yet caught the disorder from their sibling. This boy was not familiar with the term "autism," but instead described his brother as "wacky."

> **Interviewer:** Do you know if it [autism] is catching? If M. has something that makes him not able to talk and act "wacky" sometimes, can you catch it?
> **Sibling:** Yeah.
> **Interviewer:** You could? How would you catch it?
> **Sibling:** By staying too close to him.
> **Interviewer:** So, if you're too close to him for a long time, you could get "wacky" too.
> **Sibling:** Yeah.
> **Interviewer:** Do you know anybody that ever happened to?
> **Sibling:** Ummm, no.
> **Interviewer:** Is there any way that you can keep from getting "wacky" like that too?
> **Sibling:** Uh, by not staying too close to him.
> **Interviewer:** You stay close to him a lot, right?
> **Sibling:** Yeah.
> **Interviewer:** Do you worry about that sometimes, that you could catch it?
> **Sibling:** Mmmmmmm....no. 'Cause I'm always in school.
> **Interviewer:** Because of what?
> **Sibling:** 'Cause I'm always in school and he comes home before me.
> **Interviewer:** So, you're not close to him ["often"?] enough to catch it?
> **Sibling:** No.
> **Interviewer:** But if you were home all day with him, then you could catch it?
> **Sibling:** Yeah.

This child's reasoning provides an excellent example of the detailed myths that a sibling might create when factual information was either not offered or not understood. However, a sibling might also hold a less detailed belief. Consider the following excerpt from an interview with a sibling who had just turned five years old:

> **Interviewer:** Do you know if it [autism] is contagious? Can you catch it?
> **Sibling:** Yes.
> **Interviewer:** You can catch it? And what happens if you catch it?
> **Sibling:** If you catch it, that means you are autism, and if you catch it, that means that you are three years old and you like to be in that school.
> **Interviewer:** Anything else?
> **Sibling:** Um, no.
> **Interviewer:** Can you do something to keep from catching it? Can you do something so that you can't get it?
> **Sibling:** Yeah.
> **Interviewer:** What can you do?
> **Sibling:** You can stay away from it.
> **Interviewer:** So, do you have to stay away from your sister so that you don't catch it?
> **Sibling:** Yeah.

For both of the siblings described above, providing accurate, developmentally appropriate information may increase the amount of time that they spend with their brother or sister with ASD. In turn, this may allow for more opportunities for mutually reinforcing interactions.

In a recent study by Campbell and Barger (2011) involving over 1000 middle school students, approximately 5 percent of students also believed that autism was contagious. While this is a lower number than that found in the Glasberg (2000) study, it is still a surprisingly high percentage given the age of these students and the fact all participants came from schools in which some inclusive education took place. These middle-schoolers held other misconceptions, too. For example, as many as 6 percent believed that having ASD lasts about a week. While it is tempting to think the misinformation might be related to being a sibling, these data suggest that something about the disorder itself might be difficult to grasp.

You may recall that Glasberg (2000) aimed to study not just factual understanding of ASD, but, also, the level of complexity with which the siblings thought about ASD. This, in turn, would provide guidance to parents and professionals about the kinds of information that might benefit siblings at different ages. To this end, participating siblings were grouped by age and their responses were evaluated according to the categories of understanding of illness described above. Would the siblings of individuals with ASD respond similarly to the children describing health and illness concepts? Could we use those guidelines as a guide for how siblings might think about a developmental challenge, like ASD?

Changes across Developmental Stages

In attempting to learn how children think about autism, the most central questions we asked were, "What is autism" and "How do you get it?" Some findings were in-line with expectations, while other findings were more surprising. As might be predicted by their age, five- and six-year-olds typically responded to questions demonstrating reasoning that fell within the "phenomenism" stage. This type of reasoning relies very heavily on what has been seen or heard and often involves a focus on one very concrete and observable symptom. Most of the children who demonstrated this type of reasoning identified their sibling's language delay as the key symptom. The following definition of autism provided by a six-year-old girl illustrates a typical response to this question:

Interviewer: The first question that I've got to ask you about is if you ever heard the word "autism"?
Sibling: No.
Interviewer: No, you never heard of it? That's okay. Do you know why M. went to a different school?
Sibling: Yes, I know the name of it.
Interviewer: What's that?
Sibling: Douglass School.
Interviewer: That's right, remember he used to have to go there, where I worked, right? And do you know why he had to go to that special school?
Sibling: So he could learn to talk.
Interviewer: Mmm-hmm. Did he need to learn anything else??
Sibling: No.

To this young girl, ASD simply means that you need help learning to talk. This one feature of the disability had taken on the meaning of the disability itself.

You may recall that, according to research findings summarizing children's understanding of illness, siblings in middle childhood (seven- through ten-year-olds) were expected to incorporate logic and reasoning into their thinking about autism. Nevertheless, despite these expectations, these participants typically continued to use only slightly more advanced reasoning strategies than their younger counterparts. These children, as a group, used reasoning that fell within the "contagion" stage, using almost magical reasoning about illness transmission. The comments of the eight-year-old boy above who explained that he would catch autism from his brother if he spent more time at home (near his brother) and less time at school (away from his brother) exemplify contagion-based reasoning. While this way of thinking might have been predicted for young children, we had expected more advanced responses from this middle group of children.

The developmental level of responses provided by the adolescent group provided the biggest surprise. While expected to be using adult-style reasoning based on illness research, these teens' responses did not differ significantly from those in the younger two age groups. Although the language and general content of their responses sounded more sophisticated, a closer look indicated that the developmental level framing the information was still limited. Consider the following example from an interview with a thirteen-year-old girl. Like the six-year-old above, who boils down her brother's disability to not being able to talk, this thirteen-year-old uses more grown up language to say basically the same thing:

> **Interviewer:** The first question is: Have you ever heard the word "autism"?
>
> **Sibling:** Yes.
>
> **Interviewer:** Can you tell me a little bit about it?

Sibling: It's a disability that makes problems with language, and it causes children to, like, say stuff over and over. So, it's about their communication, like it's really hard for them.
Interviewer: So, the way that you would say that autism makes kids act differently is their language, communication. Anything else?
Sibling: It slows development.
Interviewer: Okay, so you said it slows development. In what way?
Sibling: It slows down, just like, language and how you learn to talk.

To sum up, the average response from children in each of the three age groups resembled one another. We did not see the large jumps in the complexity of understanding that we would expect. The older children, as a group, did not think about ASD in a significantly more sophisticated way than their young counterparts. While individual children may have responded with extreme maturity, as a group, the siblings got "stuck" thinking about ASD using reasoning typical of very young children. Again, this finding echoes those of earlier studies of siblings of children with other illnesses who actually thought about illness in a less mature manner than their peers (Carandang et al., 1979). However, because in this study we have no comparison group of children with unaffected siblings, there is no way to be sure that this gap between expected and actual understanding is unique to siblings. Instead, this could be a byproduct of the fact that autism is associated with more abstract symptoms than most other illnesses and disorders.

There are a number of reasons that a sibling might not think about their brother or sister's illness or developmental problem with any great complexity. First, the siblings may be processing information on an emotional level, which might make their thinking less mature. It may have a protective function. A second possibility might lie in parents attempting to protect their typically developing children by sharing information in limited ways. A third possibility might center on effects of a Broader Autism Phenotype (BAP), referred to in Chapter 1, encompassing language and processing deficits. As a result, we may be seeing more limited reasoning abilities in siblings. However, looking ahead in this chapter, we will soon see that while siblings had difficulty understanding the diagnosis itself, they had no delays in reasoning about the impact ASD had on their families. This debunks the possibility of broader limitations in reasoning.

It is also important to remember that our normative data from middle-schoolers (Campbell & Barger, 2011) suggests that many children share at least the misconceptions that we see among siblings. It might be that something about the nature of ASD makes it more difficult to process. The nonphysical nature of the disorder certainly makes it more confusing. You can't see if a person has it, or even do a blood test for it. It stands to reason that a lack of social skills would be harder to fully comprehend than a broken leg or the flu.

Finally, it is also useful to remember that just because a child is capable of reasoning about autism at a more sophisticated level does not mean that she has more accurate information to start with. Even siblings who are reasoning at or above the developmental level that would be predicted by their chronological age may hold misinformation or create their own autism myths. For example, in the following explanation provided by a six-year-old as to how her brother contracted autism, she utilizes a reasoning style more typical of an older child but still comes to a very inaccurate conclusion:

> *"When they're born, anybody, each kid that is autistic, they keep falling, in their mom's stomach, and then they're born. All the doctors put something around their neck and that is what makes them autistic. It's like they're bad doctors....By when they are born, they keep trying in the stomach, then when they are ready, and they want to come out, they get thrown around, and the doctors put a little something on their neck...they didn't do it to me because I was just crying, and I was so quiet, I went like this (soft cry noise). Because he was crying (loud cry noise), they put that so he could be autistic....I was talking but he can't because the doctors are so mean."*

Although some parents, like those of the girl described above, were surprised by the content of their child's responses, as a group, parents were keenly aware of the type of reasoning framing their child's thoughts. Their descriptions of how their child might respond to the interview questions typically fell within the same developmental level as their child's actual answer; yet, the facts included in the answer might not match what parents had expected. In other words, parents weren't always sure about *what* their child thought, but they were good at predicting *how* he or she would think about it. This is a heartening finding in that, as a group, parents would be pretty good at figuring out the right types of information to share with their child.

Thinking about the Implications of Autism

As predicted by their chronological age, siblings in the youngest age group (five- and six-year-olds) thought only in terms of their own, idiosyncratic experiences, and were not yet logically relating one observation to another. They also continued to focus predominantly on one symptom. The following excerpt taken from an interview with a five-year-old neurotypical sister illustrates this type of reasoning:

Interviewer: What kind of things could your brother do if he didn't have autism?
Sibling: Know how to write with pencils the right way.
Interviewer: Anything else?
Sibling: How to write the whole letters of the alphabet.
Interviewer: What else?
Sibling: He can know how to write people with pencils.

Clearly, this little girl was most struck by her brother's inability to write. This implication of the disability was her primary focus, and seems tied to her own unique experiences.

In contrast, seven- through ten-year-olds typically offered more logical descriptions of the implications of ASD based on the linking of varied observations and experiences. This concrete reasoning is exactly what would be expected for children in this group based on their chronological age. For example, an eight-year-old offered the following description of the impact of ASD on her brother's life:

"He has to go to one of those schools where people have to help them, and he has to go to a whole different place—he has to go to the (rehabilitation hospital) and Easter Seals, and he has to go the (learning center). Sometimes we used to have his therapy, they would make him ride on this scooter board. Ummmm, he would ride it through the hall, and he was very good when we would play "roll the ball" with him. I would sit on one side and he would sit on the other. He would just like bounce it a little bit over and sometimes throw it. He rolls it sometimes. It's to make him feel greater, and feel it all around his body."

This young girl is still relying on actual experiences in developing her concept of the impact of ASD, yet she is now able to tie separate events together within one larger category.

The oldest age group, eleven- through seventeen-year-olds, typically demonstrated adult reasoning when evaluating the effects of ASD. Children in this age group not only reasoned logically about past and present events, but also could evaluate the impact of ASD on hypothetical situations that had not yet occurred. Compare the following response of a seventeen-year-old girl to the question of how autism affects her brother's life to the above response from the eight-year-old:

"Um, I think it makes it different whereas he won't really ever have a normal life. He won't really like it if he stayed the way he is, he won't get to go to kindergarten or first grade. He won't, um, get to go to his high school junior prom. He won't like get to go out with his friends. He won't experience a normal life. He won't go out and feel like what it feels like to do normal things with your friends, excitement, different things, like what a book is, how you can get excited driving—go out and do the regular world. Just like normal things we get to do every day. And it will always be difficult, because my parents have told me that no matter what, T. will always have, will always be autistic and will always have that struggle. Whereas, somebody like me, things that I take for granted, like just going, going off and doing something with my friends, or like excitement, excitement over graduation—he won't ever have that."

This adolescent has taken her observations of her brother's current behaviors and experiences, and generalized from them to imagine possible and future scenarios. This sharply contrasts with the reasoning used by the younger sibling, whose thinking remains dependent upon her past experiences.

In contrast to how they described the definition and causes of autism, all three age groups performed within the expected developmental ranges when talking about the implications of autism. One possible explanation for this contrasting performance is the difference in the two topics. Siblings do not often hear people describing ASD, nor can they see or name a body part responsible for interpersonal relatedness. However, they experience the implications of autism every day. They see what other children can do and know what their sibling cannot do. They hear their parents apologizing that they cannot attend a soccer

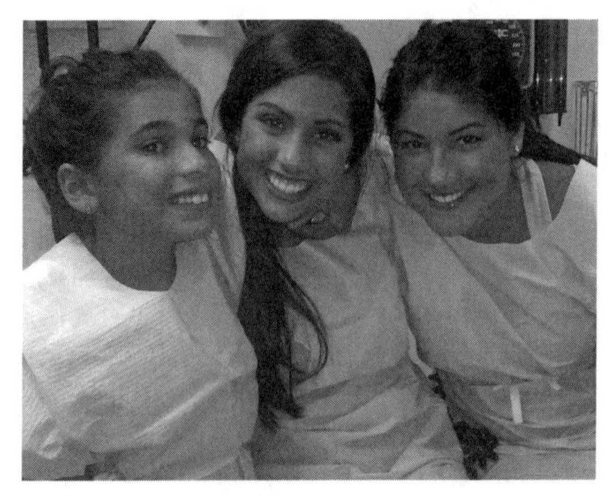

game because it is so hard to get childcare for their brother. They face questions from friends and may have to make decisions about whether or not to have friends over where they can see what goes on at home, and may even be in danger if their sibling has severe behaviors. The concrete, observable nature of this topic may make it easier for siblings of all ages to undertsand.

Interestingly, while the parents in the study were very accurate in predicting their child's understanding of the definition and causes of ASD, parents consistently overestimated their child's understanding of the implications of autism. They thought that even their very young, typically developing children might grasp the impact of their brother or sister's developmental disability on the future and on new situations that hadn't yet been experienced. In reality, this abstract and complex reasoning doesn't emerge for most children until the teenage years. This tendency to overestimate the typically developing sibling's ability to fully understand the impact of ASD is particularly striking because it means that on the one hand, parents knew that their children's understanding of the definition and causes of autism was at a less mature developmental level than would be expected based on age. But on the other hand, parents expected that their children's understanding of the implications of ASD would be more advanced than expected based on their children's age. Thus, the gap between parent's expectations for their children's development in these two areas is particularly wide. It's like the parents are saying, "My child doesn't quite get what that thing is that her sibling has, but she knows that it will forever change our lives."

What Do Your Children Think About Autism?

Many parents reading this chapter may begin to wonder about their own child's understanding of their brother or sister's ASD. You may ask questions like, "Is she thinking she might catch autism?" or "Does she understand why all of these adults come in our house and go straight for her brother?" There is only one way to find out for sure: ask! And don't be surprised if the answer you get today differs from the answer that you get next week. That is why we recommend that parents speak about ASD freely and openly, and think aloud about ASD-related topics as they come up. This creates an open door policy for discussions about autism, even for young children. Ideally, this will lead your typically developing child to ask questions as they arise, or think aloud as well. This way parents will have to do less wondering about what their child might be thinking.

Just as parents might translate other abstract information, such as religion or complex science, into the language of early childhood, so too should concepts related to ASD be translated. Even if you are pretty sure that your seven-year-old knows that her brother with severe ASD will not be in the same second grade class as she is the following year, it might help to point it out to ensure that you are helping her grasp the impact of ASD. For example, you might say something like, "Too bad Johnny won't have Mrs. Jones as a teacher next year. I really think you had a great year with her. But, she doesn't teach the smaller classes that your brother needs to be in."

While any conversation about the topic is better than none at all, try to steer away from the one-time, sit-down discussion and explanation. Because of the developmental considerations described earlier in the chapter, having "the big talk" will probably lead to confusion. Mom and Dad might think the topic has been covered, but the sibling's changing ways of seeing the world will lead to a constantly changing point of emphasis and ever-evolving questions.

Instead, make ASD as acceptable to discuss as what will be served for dinner. Try to jump in and offer brief concrete explanations of any unusual behaviors or treatments even before your child asks. Model your own confusion. For example, don't be afraid to say out loud that you wish you knew if your preschooler would ever attend the same school as your typically developing child but you just don't know. While you don't want to allow ASD to become a constant topic permeating all discussions, you also want to ensure that your children have someplace to turn with questions and feelings.

If your family has shunned the topic of ASD in the past, it may be tough to know how to suddenly introduce it. Consider using the questions and interview procedures described in this study along with these tips:

- *Hear your child out* through her whole explanation before correcting any errors.
- *Stay neutral,* regardless of what you hear—remember not to judge your child's answers.
- *Be sure to praise your child for sharing her feelings* with you.
- *Keep in mind that you want your child to feel comfortable* speaking with you again.
- *Be prepared for your child to share intense emotions from sympathy to guilt to anger.* Again, be sure to remain neutral. Your demonstration that she is entitled to whatever feelings she has may prevent her from judging herself about these feelings. Keep in mind that as your child is provided with opportunities to communicate with you, her feelings are likely to grow more positive.
- *Consider the following example* of how a parent might get a conversation like this started: "I see that, because of her special needs, we sometimes have to organize a lot of what we do around Janie. But, I realized that we've never spent much time talking about that. I want to make sure that I really understand what you are thinking and feeling about that. Do you know what her disability is called?"

What about Your Child with ASD?

Unfortunately, the reasoning of a child with ASD *about* ASD remains largely unexplored. If you have a higher functioning child with autism, however, you may be faced with the challenge of explaining ASD to her. You may wish to begin by finding out what your child currently understands. Consider using the interviewing strategies described above. Once you know how your child is currently processing ASD-related information, you will have a better understanding of the types of information that you might provide that will make the most sense to your child. For example, if she is reasoning like a younger child, then providing concrete information about her symptoms and how they affect her may be enough. If she is using more advanced reasoning and questioning the impact on future events such as getting a driver's license or having a boyfriend one day, then you can share information in a way that requires some logic and anticipation of possible situations (e.g., "The skills that you need to get a driver's license include following the road signs and traffic signals, checking the faces and gestures of other drivers and pedestrians, and passing both a written and driver's test. Let's make a list of ways that we can practice these skills to get you ready.")

The provision of accurate information at an appropriate developmental level will definitely be worth the wait. Finally, as noted above in regard to siblings, be prepared for the possibility of intense feelings associated with this topic. Your child with ASD will need your love and support as she develops an understanding of this difficult disability.

Closing Comments

Children process information differently at different ages. This holds true for siblings of children with ASD struggling to understand their brother or sister's diagnosis just as it does for other children grappling with other concepts. These developmental influences may lead siblings to misconstrue information they hear or create their own explanations for events in the absence of understandable information. To combat this, parents can engage in frequent and open conversations with their children, taking care to present information in a way that best matches their children's developmental level.

Because development is an ongoing process, the ways that your children process autism related information will keep changing, as will the questions that they ask. By creating an environment in which open dialogue about ASD is ongoing, siblings will be more likely to share ideas, questions, and comments as they arise. The next two chapters provide in-depth information about how to go about creating such an environment, as well as how to provide siblings with developmentally appropriate information.

Why Does He Do That? Explaining Autism to Children

The Mitchell Family

Laura Mitchell picked up her nine-year-old daughter, Riley, from the school's aftercare program. Riley hadn't even finished buckling her seatbelt when she blurted out, "Did you know that Carter is not retarded?"

"What!? Of course he is not retarded! Your brother reads three grades above grade level. What made you think he was retarded?"

"Well," Riley retorted, "something is wrong with him. The kids at school sometimes call him...you know, so I just figured...."

Laura fought to keep back the tears. As a single mom, it was all Laura could do to put food on the table, fight the insurance company to pay for all of Carter's therapies, and get trained on strategies to help Carter. In all of the hubbub, she really hadn't thought too much about explaining things to Riley. After all, Carter was mainstreamed. Was his disability really that obvious?

"Mom, I don't know how to break this to you, but I think Carter has Autism Spectrum Disorder." Now, Laura had known this for a long time, but where had Riley gotten this from?

"Honey, who told you that?"

"We had a speaker at school for Autism Awareness Month. She talked about kids who just aren't wired to understand other people very well, and I thought it sounded like Carter. What do you think?"

Poor Laura was not sure what to say, or where to begin.

Introduction

Laura Mitchell was stunned to suddenly learn about the questions, concerns, and conclusions that Riley had about her brother with autism. But Laura is not the first parent to be caught off guard by her typically developing child's perspective. Time and time again we hear from parents that they have learned of their child's worries or misconceptions through overhearing conversations with friends, discussions related to school papers, or even through a child's Facebook page. We have met with parents who discovered that their children thought that they caused their siblings' autism by being born first and "taking all of the good genes," or by being too loud while their mother was pregnant. And we have heard from siblings who told their parents they assumed that the autism would automatically go away by a certain age. In all of these examples, the parents had learned about these misconceptions almost by accident.

As we saw in Chapter 2, misconceptions are not uncommon for siblings of children with ASD. This is unfortunate, because the right information can act as a strong buffer against the more stressful aspects of having a sibling with ASD. First of all, as we saw with Riley, kids will fill an information vacuum with *something*. Best case scenario, siblings without information from parents will find a reasonable source, like a teacher, guidance counselor, or family friend to provide answers to their questions. Worst case scenario, a sibling, like Riley, will gather information from the taunts of peers. Access to accurate and age-appropriate information can help prevent these types of negative assumptions.

Information can also empower siblings to know how to respond to unfriendly taunts. When a gas station attendant was deriding her brother's loud behaviors in the backseat of the car while pumping gas, one sibling I know shouted at him, "My brother has autism, what is *your* problem?" In fact, various advocacy groups have printed this quote on index cards, with an explanation of ASD on the back, for people to hand out to strangers when it's difficult to respond verbally. Unfortunately, there will always be people who cause your children confusion and concern. However, it will be easier for your typically developing child to bear and challenge prejudice when he feels self-confident in his knowledge of his sibling's disability. Riley had no defense against the taunts of her peers, because she, herself, didn't understand Carter's ASD.

Information can also help siblings allay their own anxieties. As discussed in Chapter 2, the questions that might cross a sibling's mind at any age are all but endless. Can I catch autism? Will I wake up with it one day? Will my children have autism? What will happen if I go to college out of state? How can I have a boyfriend over—will he understand? And so on. Sharing information can prevent unnecessarily negative responses on the part of your sibling (e.g., staying away from one's brother with autism to avoid catching it). As Debra Lobato (1990) explains, when faced with a gap in information, whatever a child will make up is almost guaranteed to be worse than the truth.

Ignorance about autism can breed fear, and fear can damage a child's sense of himself and his relationship with his brother or sister. For example, a brother might tease his sister with ASD, as he would any other child, and then feel conscience-stricken over mistreating her. Similarly, he might feel guilty about jealous or angry reactions to his sister. He needs to know what ASD is and to understand his responses to his sister's condition, so he will be at ease with himself and with her.

To help your children be well informed about autism, accept themselves and their sibling, and fend for themselves in the world of childhood, you must be able to discuss the disorder in a way that is meaningful to the child. Precisely how you do that will vary with your child's stage of development. Chapter 2 described the limits to children's ability to comprehend abstract information when they are younger. This chapter addresses how to explain ASD to children at varying ages and stages.

How to Talk to Kids about ASD

As we saw in Chapter 2, what parents say and what children hear are two different things. Unfortunately, this can set parents up for a false sense of security. Parents who have told their typically developing

child about ASD at a young age and heard him announce to friends "My brother has autism" may believe that they have established an open atmosphere in which there are no secrets, and that the children are fully informed about ASD. It may then be puzzling when they discover that their child seems misinformed or confused about the disorder.

Psychologists who study child development would not be surprised that a child could grow up with the word autism as a household term and still not understand what it is about. Children are able to use words well before they understand them, and a boy of three or four years who says that his sister has ASD may mean no more by that than that she stares at lights or does not talk. The concept of autism is quite abstract and will not be fully understood by a child until a much older age. As a result, it is important to present the information you share with children in ways that are developmentally appropriate, and to repeat the information many times over the years, in increasingly mature and complex language, as the child grows up. These lessons about autism are to be taught many times. Try using the strategies below to communicate effectively:

1. Keep it Simple

You might recall from Chapter 2 that young children are most concerned with the concrete, the here and the now. At this young age, kids are trying to make sense of the world in general. The two-year-old is focused on questions of "what" and may endlessly ask for names of objects. Very young children will only understand autism in relation to specific, concrete behaviors. For a child this age, ASD is lining up all the toy cars in a row, throwing cereal on the floor, or riding in a yellow school bus. Although you might speak of ASD in a conversation with a child this young, he has no ability to fully understand it. His world is focused on specific behaviors and he will respond to those behaviors, positive and negative, as they occur.

By the time a child is about four years old, he will begin to be able to articulate his questions. In fact, at that age, it might seem like the questions will go on forever! Some of these questions will probably center on what the sibling personally experiences with his brother or sister. You might expect questions like, "Why doesn't my brother talk?" or "Why does he flap his hands?" If your child asks a question, simply answer the question but don't make the mistake of sharing too much information at once. A child this age will likely be best satisfied with the most concrete explanations. For example, "He can't talk now because he is still learning how," or "He flaps his hands because he thinks it is fun." These simple explanations are specific, factual, and concrete. A more extended discussion of autism will not satisfy your child's original question, and you will probably lose his attention and/or comprehension. If your child has more questions, he will ask. By simply answering and demystifying his first question, the parent has communicated that questions are okay. This will encourage more questions as they arise. Keep in mind, however, that while these simple explanations will be satisfying for the typically developing child in the short term, this does not imply any sort of deeper understanding of what ASD entails.

In addition to answering your child's questions, occasionally think up your own questions and ask them aloud. This will serve as a reminder that questioning ASD-related behaviors is okay. And it is okay to do this questioning out loud. Offer information as questions arise, mention the topic of autism from time to time, but do not overdo the educating. You can tell if your child has had enough of your question or their question by how he behaves. Is he asking questions? Nodding as you speak? Interrupting you with his own thoughts and ideas? If so, keep talking. On the other hand, is he changing the topic? Inching out of the room? Asking if you are done yet? If so, stop talking about it. We don't want the topic to become aversive.

Similarly, the same strategies for sharing information will benefit your young child with ASD if he should begin to ask questions about differences he notices in his own life. A series of quick and practical responses will lead to a much more thorough understanding than an intensive lecture at this age.

As the child enters middle childhood, he begins to logically connect his experiences. These connections may be correct or not. It is not uncommon to hear children at this age confidently asserting inaccurate facts, for example, "Whichever child is taller must be older" or "Only very old people use canes." As noted in the Glasberg study, siblings start to use logic (accurate or inaccurate) to connect their experiences about the impact of autism. As a group, however, the siblings in the Glasberg study did not demonstrate this logical reasoning and connections about ASD itself. It may help for parents to model these connections. For example, a parent might say, "Because Carl likes cars, we will stop at the car dealer as a prize for his hard work during his session today. You know, most kids his age wouldn't consider it a big thrill to go to the car dealer, but most kids his age don't like flapping their hands either! The autism makes Carl have fun different ways from other kids, but as long as he is having fun, I don't see the harm in it." This will help the child understand how all their observations feed into one disorder.

A higher functioning child with ASD in this age group will also benefit from a parent highlighting logical connections between experiences. Any insight a child on the spectrum can gain will only lead to self-management. A parent might say something like, "I know it's hard for you sometimes because you are the only student in your class interested in fonts. But it's just like when you were very interested in talking about flags. You just have to hang on to the information until you can either find a friend with a common interest or until you get home to me."

You might also recall from Chapter 2 that even older siblings used fairly basic reasoning when thinking about ASD. Nothing will be gained by offering highly complex information all at once to a child of any age. Offer brief, but clear, explanations and comments, and always invite more conversation on the subject. This will ensure that your child gets what he needs. If he wants more, he knows that he can ask. Again, this strategy should be generalized to sharing information about ASD with your child with ASD.

Table 3-1 | Telling Your Child about Autism

In Early Childhood

- You can't catch autism.
- It is nobody's fault.
- He hasn't learned how to talk yet.
- I will keep you safe.

In Middle Childhood

- Autism happens before a person is born or when he is a baby.
- It is a difference in the brain.
- It can make it hard to learn to talk, play, or understand other people's feelings.
- People with autism can learn, but we have to find the right way to teach them, which sometimes takes a while.
- If your brother is aggressive, it's my job to keep everyone safe, not yours.
- You can help him by playing and showing him how to do things.
- If your friends have questions, I can help you figure out what to say.

2. *Safety First*

Younger children have a strong need to feel safe. Because individuals with ASD may exhibit self-destructive or aggressive behaviors, young siblings may observe behaviors that are scary and possibly dangerous on a daily basis. Even stereotypic behaviors, like rocking or flapping, can be confusing or unsettling to a young observer. In fact, these behaviors can be a source of distress for the entire family. Very young children, in particular, may observe their parents' distress and have an emotional response to it, before they are able to articulate their questions and concerns.

Depending on the nature of the challenging behaviors, older siblings may also need some reassurance for their safety. Unfortunately, stories that involve injury or bodily harm, even to parents, are not that rare. The anxiety some children may feel for their safety may sadly be a valid concern. For this reason, and the strain of straddling the role between parent and sibling, we recommend that siblings are not asked to manage disruptive behaviors, not even older siblings. Siblings may provide positive reinforcement for appropriate behaviors, or deliver mild discipline such as saying "no," but most siblings will be neither emotionally nor physically prepared to use stronger procedures such as restraint, or even removal of a reinforcer if a physical altercation is probable. While a teen may be left in charge of a very young sibling or an older sibling who does not engage in aggressive or self-injurious behaviors, a teen should never be left in charge of an older or larger sibling who might place both children in danger.

In these situations, wordy explanations will be unlikely to be effective. However, concrete intervention and simple words may help. For example, if your son is frightened by his sister's tantrums, he must be comforted and reassured. He also must be given a safety plan. Maybe your son can be taught to go get mom and leave the room if his sister exhibits certain early signs of agitation? Maybe he can go to his bedroom and close the door until you tell him it is safe to come out? The most important part is that he knows what to do in the situation and feels confident that he can keep himself safe, and that his parents will keep him safe.

A child will also need to know that his brother or sister is safe. Keep in mind that watching the consequences for behavior problems can be frightening as well. For example, although a proper restraint will not hurt a child engaged in a challenging behavior, it might look very scary to a young onlooker. It will be important to let the child know that it doesn't hurt. At another time, it might even be helpful to offer to place the typically developing sibling in the specific hold to demonstrate what the child with ASD is experiencing.

Even the child on the spectrum who may be engaging in unsafe behaviors may need a reminder that you will keep him safe. At times, individuals with ASD engage in challenging behaviors impulsively, or during a period in which they feel that they have lost control. The parent will want to discuss safety measures, even with the child causing the dangerous situation. This may calm his anxiety, and may ultimately help prevent the behavior all together.

3. *Feelings Matter*

Just as young children are "in the moment" in terms of thoughts, they are also "in the moment" in terms of feelings. People familiar with young children will not need to be told that no amount of logic or reasoning will deter them from feeling angry if they can't have what they want, feeling jealous if someone else has it, or feeling sad if what they want is gone. Just like any young child, siblings of children with autism will need reassurance and comfort. If your child is frightened by the odd behaviors of his older sibling, reassure him that he is safe and, again, physically remove him from the area if your child with autism is engaging in tantrums or aggressive behavior that might be harmful. It can be easy to focus on the child having the behavior problems rather than the child on the side behaving appropriately, but it can help to keep that child's perspective in mind. This is especially important with young children as they may not be able to interpret the behaviors they observe. They may even think that the behaviors are appropriate, which will set up a problem later when the younger sibling may imitate the behaviors and receive a very different response from his parents.

Although middle childhood is marked by growth in logic and reasoning, kids this age have feelings, too. While they may also be better at perceiving the relationships between their parent's behaviors and the demands of ASD, it does not mean that they won't have feelings about it. For example, a child this age may understand that play dates, homework projects, and school plays have all been interrupted by behaviors associated with ASD—and may not feel very happy about it. It will be helpful for a parent to respond to these concerns directly. He may say something like, "I know it has been hard for you that we can't really predict or prevent when Mike will have a behavior problem. We are working really hard with his behaviorist to get those problems to stop. In the meantime, we are going to try to get babysitters when you have something special going on, and we are going to get a lock on your door so that you can keep special things safe." And, importantly, follow up by checking in. A question like, "Do you think that will do the trick?" or "What else might help?" is critical. This helps the child know that their input is welcome, and the doors of communication are open.

You may recall that the Glasberg study suggests that children this age still use somewhat magical reasoning when thinking about what autism is and where it comes from. Be aware that this can lead to further emotional responses associated with anxiety or guilt. One little girl in a sibling discussion group shared with us that she felt that she had caused her brother's autism by misbehaving too much when her mother was pregnant. To make up for this, she was trying to save up all of her money to order special "holy water" that she had seen advertised in a magazine, with the hopes that it would cure her brother.

Parents may need to reassure children about possible fears. Just as we need to show them that there are no monsters under the bed, we need to assure them that nothing magical will occur or has occurred to hurt the child or his sibling. We need to correct their mistaken logic, giving them the simple facts they need such as that they cannot catch autism as they might catch a cold. Because children may or may not have these concerns, and may or may not voice these concerns, it can be hard for a parent to know what to discuss. The key is to create open lines of communication to ensure that the child knows no question is off limits, and any question will be heard. Modeling by sharing one's own thoughts can start a wonderful dialogue. For example, when a mother sees her child with autism engaged in stereotypic behavior, she might say aloud, "I really wish that Joey would just play with toys like other kids. I used to think that maybe I did something to make him struggle like this, but I am very clear now that this is just something he was born with."

Older children will have complicated emotions around ASD. Recall, from the Glasberg study, that siblings at this age not only understand what has happened already, but also understand what might happen in the future. This can create a bevy of questions, like, who will care for their brother or sister with ASD when the parents no longer can? If ASD comes from genetics, will the sibling's own children have ASD? How independent will their brother or sister with ASD be able to become? To prevent this type of reasoning from becoming anxiety-provoking, your teenaged children should have access to as much information about ASD as they wish. But, keep in mind, the Glasberg study also showed that these siblings, on the whole, may not process factual information about the disorder as maturely as they process information about the implications of ASD. Parents may be surprised at the support their teens need in developing a mature understanding of ASD. Again, open lines of communication coupled with parents modeling discussion of their own feelings will encourage teens to share their questions and feelings as well.

Because individuals with ASD vary so widely in terms of their facility in expressing and understanding feelings, it is hard to say whether or not these strategies will be helpful for the individual with ASD himself. However, certainly labeling and modeling your own emotional responses and those of siblings can only help that child's skills improve.

4. Offer Creative Outlets

In sibling discussion groups, kids are provided with a variety of crafts and activities designed to help them express their feelings. Why not do these activities at home? For example, you might consider creating a book about ASD with your typically developing child. This will help you identify your child's conceptions and misconceptions, and allow a forum for discussion. Even a young child can dictate the text and illustrate the book with pictures from magazines. This book might be presented to the child's class, shared with family members, or left on the coffee table to address questions from visitors. Alternatively, it might be kept in a drawer for only the sibling to access when needed, if that is what your child finds more comforting. Other ideas might include reading books about ASD together (see "Books about ASD and Special Needs for Siblings" in the Resource Guide at the back of this book) and writing letters to one or more of the characters, or creating a comic strip about ASD. For more ideas to help children talk about their brother or sister's disability, explore Meyer and Vadasy's (2008) *Sibshops* book, or visit http://siblingsupport.org/.

Some siblings benefit from creative outlets that have nothing to do with ASD. Many siblings have shared with us that their time spent in competitive dance, or on a traveling soccer team, or in Boy Scouts is sacred to them as time that is truly theirs. It is a time of their day that is about them, and does not require them to take a backseat to anyone else. They can focus their mind on what most interests them, which many siblings find rejuvenating. Supporting these interests to the extent possible can be very helpful for siblings.

5. Help Them Find Their Own Way

As you may have already noticed, some siblings gain strength from immersing themselves in the family and in issues related to ASD. This may be why we find an overrepresentation of adult siblings of individuals with special needs in helping professions (e.g., Strohm, 2005). Other siblings find their strength through developing separate spaces for themselves. Every brother or sister of an individual with autism will respond to the experience in a different way. Some siblings won't go to college out of state because they fear their parents will not be able to manage on their own; others feel the best way to honor their parents is to assure them that their lives will not be limited by their brother or sister's diagnosis. It is important for parents to acknowledge that these decisions are the siblings' decisions to make. No one benefits when an individual is forced into a role that he is not comfortable with—there are always solutions that can be found that respect each individual's right to chart his own life course.

Although we often think of adolescent decisions about questions such as how far to move from their parents, as decisions that might come up in the teen years, these choices begin with small steps in middle childhood. Will the sibling take or be given the time to participate in an after school club? Will he bring friends to the house or channel play dates predominantly outside the home? Will he choose friends around tolerance or escape from the challenges of ASD? As a parent, allowing a child to explore the larger world at this stage will help the child discover his own identity, skills, and interests, which will provide the confidence and experience to make larger decisions around independence as he gets older.

6. *Cherish Mediocrity*

In our work with siblings over the years, we repeatedly see kids who express some self-assigned pressure to assume an extreme role. Some kids explicitly aim for "superbad." They share very openly with us that they believe if they do not misbehave, they will not get any attention. Other kids describe pressure to go the exact opposite direction. They explain that they feel the need to be as perfect as possible. They perceive their parents to have a great deal on their plate due to their brother or sister with ASD, and don't want to add to their burden. The pressure and consequences from either extreme are draining on the sibling.

You might recall from Chapter 1 that, on average, siblings of children with ASD fall within the normal range for both acting out behaviors (externalizing) and negative feelings (internalizing) on standardized assessments. However, more individual siblings of children with ASD got scores on these assessments that indicated a concerning level of internalizing and/or externalizing problems. This suggests that while some siblings had extremely concerning scores, other siblings must have had almost no behavioral concerns at all to bring the group scores back into the average range (Rodrigue, Geffken, & Morgan, 1993; Glasberg, 2000). This reflects what we observed clinically, that siblings are often choosing between behavioral extremes. Some siblings are working very hard not to distract their already overtaxed parents, while others might use challenging behaviors to cry out for attention.

Thankfully, the vast majority of siblings we meet are comfortably in the middle—having challenges as they naturally arise, as any child might.

In order to address this, parents can work to pay attention to everyday successes and challenges. Providing a high degree of attention to moderate behaviors may prevent the extremes. Furthermore, allow your language to reflect your acceptance of moderation. For example, a well-meaning statement about how much a parent appreciates that a sibling never has to be reminded to do his chores or his homework, and it makes her life so much easier to not have to keep such a close eye on that child, may inadvertently be giving the message that requiring the periodic reminders that most children need would present a burden. In other words, watch your language!

In addition to taking it easy on your typically developing child, take it easy on yourself. Parenting is a ridiculously hard job that comes with no manual and changes with each child. Do your best, and know that is all that you can do. Not only will you decrease the pressure on yourself by avoiding unrealistic expectations, you will also be providing a role model to your child. It is great for your child to see her parent try, and fail, sometimes. Your child will learn much more by seeing how you cope with occasionally making mistakes and admitting your imperfection than by the notion that perfect is the only acceptable standard.

Parents Speak

Over the years, my children and I have discussed Donald's disabilities many times—not so much in clinical terms, but in terms of their feelings about him. There are times we need to explain Donald's behavior to neighbors or friends and that can be difficult, especially for the children. Martha explains everything away by saying, "Donald is just handicapped." Sam will go into more detail to try to get the other person to understand Donald's difficulties. Rather than define autism, he describes Donald as the child he is.

It's a challenge to divide attention equally when sometimes one child clearly needs more attention. There's no magic bullet to dealing with this other than to try to explain what's happening to the kids. They are getting old enough now that they understand there is a difference to Jimmy and are familiar with the word autism. I think because Jimmy is the oldest (nine years old), in some respects it's easier because it's always been this way. Jimmy is mostly gentle but has bitten our middle son a couple of times. This is obviously difficult to handle. Our middle son (seven years old) is very sensitive and it's hard for him not to feel there is personal intent behind Jimmy's actions. Usually it's happened in moments when Jimmy is excited or agitated. Anyway, there's no magic bullet. We try to talk honestly to our other kids about what we know and what we don't know. We admit that we don't understand, ourselves, exactly why Jimmy is the way he is. I think that's tough for kids sometimes—they want to think adults have all the answers. But in this situation, it seems to be the right thing. And we're very proud of how they treat their brother and hope those relationships will be valuable to Jimmy throughout his life.

Today, when I stand back and take a hard look at Annie's understanding of Matt's autism, I realize it has been a gradual process for her. As early as age three, Annie questioned why Matt wouldn't answer her or play with her. I would explain to her that Matt was still "learning to talk" or still "learning to play." Then I would prompt from Matt some speech or play directed toward Annie.

As Annie grew closer to five years old, her questions regarding Matt increased and grew more complex ("Why does Matt need help talking?" and "Why can't he go to my school?"). I told her Matt had difficulty learning to speak and doing certain things because of something called "autism." I explained to her that Matt was born with autism, as were other children in his school. Annie wanted to know if he would "always be like this." I answered her by saying I didn't know exactly what Matt would be like when he was older. I did know that we would continue to work very hard with him. I told her that together we had already helped Matt so much. I let her know how very proud I was of her. I knew sometimes it was difficult for her. Matt put a lot of demands on my time, and there were times when she was in uncomfortable situations because of his behaviors. I gave her time to speak about those feelings.

Lastly, I reminded her that we were a family, and that meant she was not alone. I told her that we were fortunate to be able to talk to each other about everything, whenever we needed to. Then I said, "I love you so very much," and she repeated those words back to me and gave me her biggest hug.

Zack is only five and Jeff, who has autism, is seven. Zack asks things like why Jeff won't play with him or why he won't talk. I give him simple answers like, "He still has to learn how to talk." I hope that is enough.

We have gone through some hard times since my daughter entered junior high school. She seems to be embarrassed by me, her father, and her brother Jack. She doesn't want to be seen with Jack, whose behavior can be quite disruptive. My husband and I are thinking of some counseling for her.

I remember when I was a senior in high school and we had to do our senior term paper. I decided to write mine on what causes autism. Although I had grown up with a sister who has autism and watched my parents cope with her every day, I never really understood what made her that way. So I wrote this paper on what made people autistic. I couldn't believe some of the stuff I read about how parents made their kids that way and I got really upset. I knew my parents were too great for that. Then I found this book in the library by a guy named Bernard Rimland. It was all about how autism was probably caused by damage to the brain. That made a lot of sense to me. Remember, this was a lot of years ago, back in the late '60s, before all the great research that has been done.

Ellen is fifteen and goes to the regional high school. This year they had a class assignment in English to write about their personal hero. I was moved to tears when I read her essay. She had written about her younger brother, Seth, who is nine and has autism. She wrote about how hard he has struggled to learn to talk and how brave he seems to her, always trying to get beyond his autism.

4 Let's Talk: Helping Children Share Their Thoughts and Feelings

The Svenson Family

Roger Svenson had served two tours of duty in Iraq as a US Army staff sergeant with a military police unit. He was a member of the Army Reserve and had recently gotten notice that his unit was scheduled to go to Afghanistan to train their local police force as part of the preparation for the return of American troops to the US. Another year in a faraway nation was a major disruption to his family and his return to civilian life, but he felt the strong pull of duty to help the people of Afghanistan assume responsibility for their own futures. He and his wife, Carol, had talked at length about what this meant for the family and especially for Zack, his twelve-year-old son with an autism spectrum disorder. They were both upset about Roger's impending departure, and knew that they had to call a family meeting to tell the children what was going to happen and how the family would cope.

At dinner one night, Roger and Carol told their children there would be a family meeting ten o'clock the next morning and that everyone needed to be there. In their family, "everyone" meant Roger, Carol, twelve-year-old Zack, eight-year-old Suzanne, and five-year-old Todd. Their family dog, Ruffy, was welcome, but not required to attend!

At ten o'clock sharp, Carol called the meeting to order and told the children their father had some important news to share with them. Roger glanced around the table. Suzanne was sitting attentively and looking at her dad, Todd looked back at him with a serious expression, and Zack was gazing over his father's shoulder, but appeared alert. Roger told them that the Army needed him again for another year, but that he would be back as soon as he could. Suzanne's lower lip quivered as she fought to hold back tears, and Carol, seeing her daughter close to crying, moved her chair closer to Suzanne and put her arm around her. Todd was too young to remember the times his father had been in Iraq and could not grasp what his father meant by going away for the year. Zack, who had been through Roger's two previous deployments, began to rock in his chair.

Carol and Roger gave the children a few minutes to collect themselves and then said it was important that they talk as a family about how they were going to cope with Roger's being away for so long. Carol said she knew it would be hard for everyone, but they would all pull together as a family and get through the year. Suzanne, who loved her big brother, said "But what about Zack, he really needs Daddy to be here." Roger said that he and Carol had talked about Zack a lot because he knew their oldest boy depended on Roger a great deal.

Zack, who was a very bright boy, was identified as a child who was on the higher functioning end of the autism spectrum. He was included in a regular education class and got good grades in most of his subjects. But he really struggled with how to get along with other children. He was still learning how to approach a group of children on the playground and not disrupt what they were doing. He was getting better at asking if he could play and usually the other kids would let him be part of their games. But he was not very well coordinated, and things like throwing or kicking a ball, catching a ball in the air, or running bases were very difficult for him. He longed to be a "regular" guy, but it was very hard for him.

Roger spent a lot of time with Zack teaching him sports skills so he could keep up with the other boys and Zack was gradually getting better at his gross motor skills, but he still had a lot to learn. In response to Suzanne's question, Roger said that Uncle Bob would be coming over a couple of times each week to help Zack with his sports and he would play games with Suzanne and Todd as well. So, Zack would still get his lessons, and Suzanne and Todd would spend some special time with Uncle Bob. The children all thought Uncle Bob was a great guy, and he had even played baseball in college, so that sounded like a good idea to them.

Carol asked Zack if he understood what his dad had just said and if he thought he could learn from Uncle Bob. Zack looked away, but answered her saying he guessed it would be okay, but nobody was like his dad. Carol said she knew that their father was the best dad ever, but that Uncle Bob would be fun too.

Suzanne got teary once again and blurted, "But I'm going to miss Daddy. I don't want him to go away." That was one of the hard times in the meeting for Roger and he felt himself getting emotional as well. He said how much he loved each of them and how hard it was for him to go away, but when the Army told him he had to go, he had to obey the order even though it made him sad. Then he said he was taking his computer with him and that they would be able to see each other by video conference almost every day. Communicating this way would give them a chance to tell him what was on going on at home and show him things they had made, and that would help him feel like he was still part of the family. The children would be able to see their dad and know he was doing okay.

Toward the end of the meeting, Carol and Roger said they thought it would be nice to take a family vacation for a few days so they could spend some time together before Dad had to leave. Roger asked them where they would like to go. Carol got out a pencil and paper and wrote down their ideas. Maybe they could go to Washington, DC. How about Disneyland? See penguins in Antarctica! What about going swimming in the ocean? It was Zack who spoke up and said, "We should go camping, just like we always do. That's fun." Then, Carol said, "Okay, we have a good list now. Let's choose one." They quickly agreed that Antarctica was too far away for a short trip. After a little more discussion they all agreed that camping would be the most fun and would give them all time together before Roger left. So, it was agreed by the whole family that they would spend a few days in the mountains taking hikes and having a good time together. Todd asked if Ruffy could come along and everyone said he needed to be there. They also decided that as soon as Roger got home they would take another family trip.

Although each of them confessed they would feel sad some of the time, they promised to be good to one another and keep up their spirits while Roger was away. The children also said they would cooperate with their mother and do what Uncle Bob asked of them.

Introduction

Good communication is one of the essential elements of a happy, well-functioning family. Children and parents need to able to share their thoughts and feelings. Sometimes families do this by calling a family meeting where everyone is present and can share their ideas for a solution to a family problem or join together to make a plan for a family adventure. The meeting's aim is to find a solution that is acceptable to everyone in the family; however, this doesn't mean that everyone in the family will be perfectly satisfied with the plan. Sometimes a lot of compromise is needed. There will always be some decisions that have to be made by the adults, but children can be given a chance to voice how they feel about the plan and tell their parents what would make it easier for them to accept. This was clear in the case of the Svenson family. Roger had no choice about serving with his unit in Afghanistan, and neither he nor Carol was especially happy about his going away for another year. But they both knew it was his duty to serve and that he would do so with devotion to his responsibilities. The more abstract concepts of duty and honor that made the decision clear to them as adults were beyond the grasp of their children, and they had to give the children a forum in which to express their feelings and make suggestions about what might make the year a little easier for them.

Both Carol and Roger were especially concerned about Zack, who was bright, but not very attuned to people's feelings, and who counted on his dad to teach him how to play sports with the other kids. Zack had made some nice progress with learning the gross motor skills of sports and those skills were making it easier for him to interact with other kids on the playground. Wisely, Carol and Roger asked a family member to step in and take over Roger's coaching role with the children for the next year so progress would not be lost.

Roger and Carol were concerned about the emotional impact of Roger's leaving on all three children and the risk of resulting behavior problems. It was essential to them that Roger stay in continual touch with the family, so to ensure this they furnished Roger with a laptop with a camera so the family could communicate regularly via video conference.

Effective parenting involves teaching children the skills that result in the open exchange of ideas and problem solving. As parents, we are charged with creating the conditions that allow our children to practice these skills and integrate them into their social repertoires. Children who learn from their parents how to communicate well with people they love will find that those skills hold them in good stead all of their lives. Not only will they be happier with the family of their childhood, they should also be able to carry these same skills into their adulthood with friends and coworkers, and pass them on to their children.

Many of the conversations you have with your neurotypical children about ASD or about other topics of concern to you or your children will occur informally when something happens that triggers a discussion. Alternatively, as we just saw in the case of the Svenson family, parents may call a family meeting to share important information with everyone and give all of the family members a voice in the conversation. Carol and Roger Svenson were facing an event that would have an impact on their entire family and especially on their twelve-year-old son, Zack, who has an autism spectrum disorder.

In their family meeting, Roger and Carol shared the information about Roger's impending deployment to Afghanistan and gave the children a chance to react to that. Then, they described some of the things they were going to do to make the year as easy as possible for everyone. Finally, they asked for the children's ideas about a family trip they might take together before Roger had to leave. They all made suggestions and they all got to vote.

In this chapter, we are going to describe some of the procedures the Svenson family used to help ensure that their family meeting was an effective one. However, before we do that we want to examine some of the factors that make communication between parents and children challenging and some of the things you can do as a parent to make conversations easier. Family communication when there is a child on the autism spectrum is made especially complex because of the amount of time and extra help that the child needs. In addition, for many families, behavior management issues place extensive demands on parents and further limit their time for the rest of the family. Every family has its own style, its own customs, its own cultural understanding, and its own rituals. Learning about some of the obstacles to effective communication and some of the ways that other families overcome them may give you ideas you can adapt to your own situation.

Creating an Atmosphere for Communication

Many of us have been fortunate over the years to know a few people who seem able to look into our hearts. They might be parents, grandparents, siblings, best friends, therapists, or religious advisors. They listen closely to us, understand our words, encourage us to discover who we are, and help us understand ourselves a bit better. We flourish in these relationships, becoming more open, understanding our feelings, and gaining wisdom about ourselves and the people around us. Good parents create this kind of context; so do good friends and good psychotherapists. Love alone is not enough to accomplish that ideal. Loving your child is essential to good communication, but there are other things you need to do as well to help the sharing process.

Good listening skills are essential to creating an atmosphere where your child will feel able to reveal thoughts and feelings to you. In the following pages, we will consider both some of the barriers that make it harder for parents and children to communicate about autism spectrum disorders, and some of the specific methods you can use to help your child feel more at ease in sharing experiences and in communicating with her brother or sister on the autism spectrum. People who have used these skills tell us they are helpful not only in talking to their neurotypical children, but also with their spouse/partner, their friends, and their coworkers.

Barriers to Communication

Although most parents would like to communicate effectively with their children about a sibling's autism spectrum disorder, there can be barriers that make this sharing difficult. One barrier is the emotional reactions parents may experience about the impact of autism on the life of a cherished child. It is quite common for parents to feel such emotions as deep sadness, loss, or anger about a child's spectrum disorder. These feelings are a normal response to the tragic effect of this disorder on a child's development. We all want what is best for our children and it is painful to realize that their lives will be more of a struggle than the lives of neurotypical children.

Parents may fear revealing negative feelings to their children because they are ashamed of the feelings, think they are abnormal, or because they do not wish to burden their children with their emotions. Unfortunately it is difficult to keep our feelings secret, especially from our family members who share our home and see all of our moods on a daily basis. If you grew up in a home where one of your parents was depressed, chronically angry, or alcoholic, you know that reality was part of your own growing up. You cannot totally conceal your own feelings from your children. Although a child may not know why Dad is sad or Mom is angry, she is very likely to pick up on the feelings. She will notice the sadness in your face, the edge of anger in your voice, your lack of pleasure in the small things, or your preoccupation with your own thoughts.

Most of us cannot conceal these clues to our real feelings. Your child will notice these changes in your behavior and react to them. If she has no other explanation, she may attribute your distress to something she did, and she may begin to blame herself for some imagined offense. Every child does little things that leave her feeling guilty. These are minor infractions that do not matter to us as adults. However, in her mind these childish behaviors can loom large and be magnified into the reason that you are upset. As we described in Chapters 2 and 3, sometimes a child can frighten herself with the things she imagines.

Clearly, parents do not wish to burden children with the full intensity of their feelings of grief, anxiety, or profound disappointment about a sibling's autism spectrum disorder. Such feelings are best shared with one's partner, close friends, relatives, religious advisor, psychotherapist, or members of a parent support group. However, children can understand that their parents feel a range of emotions just as children do. They can accept that sadness, anger, or regret may be among your many reactions, along with love, concern, and other positive feelings that a parent experiences in relation to a child.

If you label your own emotions, and explain that they are linked to your concern for your child with an autism spectrum disorder, but do not diminish your love for that child or for your other children, this may help to ease your neurotypical child's concerns about your emotional state. At the very least, your child will know that she is not the cause of your distress, and she can realistically label your feelings as due to other events in your life. You should share "good" feelings as well as painful ones, both when your child comments on your behavior and when she does not. Younger children need simple labels like "happy," "sad," or "mad," while older children can deal with more complex feelings of frustration, exhilaration, or apprehension.

Although labeling feelings is important, parents are also entitled to the privacy of their own feelings, and you should respect your own needs just as you do those of your child. Share what you are able, but do not share what you need to keep private. Try to remain calm as you describe your feelings about a troubling situation, or defer the conversation until after you've regained your composure. Here is an example of appropriate sharing of adult feelings:

Mr. C had recently been so preoccupied with finding a school program that could address the disruptive behaviors of his six-year-old son with autism that he neglected to pay much attention to his twelve-year-old son. So Mr. C sent his eldest son a text message inviting him to go fishing on Saturday. They would pack a lunch, take their fishing tackle, and rent a boat at a lake where they both loved to fish.

The following week, while fishing, Mr. C and his son talked about how distracted he had been by the behavior problems of the younger son. Although Mr. C explained that the younger son's issues had been weighing heavily on him, he did not burden his eldest son with the more intense feelings he had shared with his wife and his brother-in-law. Mr. C apologized for not having paid much attention to his older boy and said that he really wanted to make a priority of spending more quality time together. He also asked his son if he had any questions and listened carefully to what the boy had to say.

In addition to wishing to protect children from their adult feelings, another obstacle to communication is a parent's desire to spare their children from having to confront the painful reality of their sibling's developmental disorder. This attempt at protection may, however, only heighten the mystery about the sibling's autism spectrum disorder. As we discussed in Chapters 2 and 3, the explanations children invent to explain their brother's or sister's behavior can be far more frightening than the realities of an autism spectrum disorder. It is therefore essential that you provide age-appropriate explanations and ensure that siblings have facts, not fantasies, about spectrum disorders. Providing this information will help children understand why their sibling on the spectrum needs more parental attention, and may serve to ease some of the jealous or resentful feelings that almost inevitably occur when a child sees her parent paying more attention to another child. The truth is almost always healthier than a fantasy your child might create to explain why you spend more time with her brother than with her.

Communication between Intimate Partners

Good communication in a family has to happen between parents as well as between parents and children. What happens between parents matters not only to those two adults, but to their children as well, as illustrated by the following story:

A mother confided to us that she was beside herself with worry about what was going to happen to her teenage son when he reached adulthood. The state they lived in had pitifully few resources for adults and her son might be on a waiting list for months or even years before he got any services. She did not feel she could discuss this with her husband who had medical problems that were a source of concern to both of them.

About a month later, we heard from this woman's husband that he was worried he might die and leave his wife to have to cope with their sometimes difficult son on her own. He wanted to be strong for his wife, but he was worried about his health and about his son. We encouraged the husband to raise these issues with his wife and to approach their state's services for adults with autism to see what kind of priority their son might have because of the husband's failing health and his inability to control his son's outbursts.

Ultimately, they were both very much relived to have the door between them open up so they could discuss their mutual concerns and begin to make plans that took everyone's needs into account. They also held a family meeting with their other adult children and shared with them their concerns about the father's health and their brother's continuing needs. The parents used this as an opportunity to learn from their two older children what they saw as their role in the future of their brother with autism and to make realistic financial plans for the family. It was not an easy conversation, but it was a very important one.

In this case, a bit of encouragement to the husband to communicate his concerns to his wife allowed the two to share their emotions and relieve some of the pressure. Further, this improvement in their communication made it possible for the family to work as a team to successfully make necessary future plans.

These principles of communication are not just for a husband and wife. Any two (or more) adults who are raising a child need to be able to talk to one another. If you are a grandparent who is helping your adult child raise her family or an uncle who has stepped in to be a "father" in a family that has lost its biological father, you will also need to become adept at this kind of communication.

Learning to communicate with your spouse or partner takes practice, trust, and effort. Few of us ever become "expert" at communication all of the time. Some general principles to follow are outlined in the section on "Skills for Communicating" below.

Some couples do very well at this kind of communication, but others may need outside help to get the process going. Consulting a professional therapist or religious advisor with counseling skills is a wise course of action if a marriage or other close childrearing relationship is especially troubled.

Communication between Children

When one child has an autism spectrum disorder, the spoken language between siblings may be very limited. This is especially true if the child on the spectrum has an intellectual disability as well as an

ASD. Under these conditions, words might be of limited value, and the child with an ASD will communicate mainly through behavior. In the case of a youngster like Zack Svenson, whom you met in the beginning of this chapter, many higher functioning children on the spectrum can communicate, yet struggle to be effective speakers. If your child with an autism spectrum disorder does not also have an intellectual disability, she might have a full vocabulary and be able to generate grammatically correct sentences, but still not be able to successfully express her feelings and reactions. This was true for Zack, who was included in regular classes in school, but had a hard time articulating his concerns about his father's impending departure. Regardless of your child's intellectual skills and position on the autism spectrum, the communication between your children may be improved if you can be sensitive to the frustration of your neurotypical children in trying to understand their sibling on the spectrum, and can provide all of the children the support they need to move communication forward.

If your child on the autism spectrum is not yet speaking, but is using an alternative form of communication, such as sign language or a Picture Exchange Communication System (Bondy & Frost, 2011), it is important that her siblings learn how to use the system as well. You may want to teach your neurotypical child some signs or pictures that are frequently used in play between the siblings. If both children share these skills, it will make it easier for them to communicate. The rudiments of these systems are easy enough for even a young child to grasp. In fact, some hearing people with typically developing infants teach their children a few simple signs to communicate their needs before they develop speech.

When your children are young, you will have to actively structure much of their communication. You can attempt to translate the behavior of your child with an autism spectrum disorder for his sister. For example, "He is ignoring you because he doesn't know how to play with that toy. Maybe you can show him how it works," or "When Jack has a tantrum, it means he is upset, but he doesn't have words to tell us that." As she gets older, your neurotypical child will learn to "read" her sibling's behavior and to interpret his language. If your child on the spectrum does have speech, she may be very adept at communicating about factual things, but be more limited in sharing feelings. You should encourage the neurotypical sibling to use her words to express her feelings to her sibling with ASD and to you.

Over time, your child with an autism spectrum disorder may become more aware of other people's feelings and may learn to label them, verbally or otherwise. Neurotypical siblings can help with that learning by labeling their own feelings. You can help facilitate this through role playing with your neurotypical child what to do when her brother with ASD does something that is upsetting. For example, your daughter might learn to say to her brother, "You made me mad when you broke my doll. I don't want to play with any more today." The calmer she can remain when she says this, the easier it may be for her brother to hear her and know he has done something wrong. You can also work with your child on the spectrum to teach him how to understand what other people may be feeling and how to apologize when he upsets someone. Understanding that someone else is upset by what we did to him is called "perspective taking," and this can be very difficult for children on the spectrum to master. You may need to work at it patiently for many years, taking advantage of all of the opportunities that come along. The book *Reaching Out, Joining In* (Weiss & Harris, 2001) discusses how to help children on the autism spectrum learn these perspective-taking skills. Psychologist Tom Buggey (2009) wrote about "self-modeling" in which parents or teachers make videos of a child performing a desired skill such as commenting on someone's feelings. That video can be viewed by the child so she can see how she behaves under the best conditions. The book has detailed instructions about how to make these useful teaching videos.

Your child with an autism spectrum disorder will probably have a great deal of difficulty understanding her neurotypical sibling. He may not follow his sister's instructions, understand that he has upset her, and may often ignore her. This ignoring, or even active avoidance, can be puzzling and upsetting to a sibling who wants to play with her brother. She yearns to have a playmate and he seems impossible to engage. Both of your children will need your help in getting beyond these barriers. Chapter 6 describes some specific things you can do as a parent to help your neurotypical child and your child on the spectrum establish communication through play.

Skills for Communicating

Open communication is important in every family, regardless of whether there is a child with an autism spectrum disorder or not. Some parents are fortunate to have grown up in families where their parents were good models of communication, while others grew up with parents who did not talk much about feelings or concerns. If you already know how to let the communication flow between you and your children, you are that much farther ahead. But, if you grew up in a family where your parents were not able to teach you effective communication skills, you can still learn them as an adult and you can share them with your own children. The most basic skill to effective communication between parents and children is good listening. That is more difficult than it sounds. Much of the time, when we have a conversation with another person, we are only partially attending to them because we are busy planning what we want to say next or how to solve the other person's problem. It takes practice to set aside that tendency and really listen to the other speaker.

Although teaching your child how to solve problems is important, many times simply hearing her out is more important. Perhaps it has been your own experience that as you talk about your concerns with a good listener, you are often able to generate your own solutions. Being able to "own" the solution to our problems is usually more satisfying than having someone else solve our problems. That means that careful listening should take precedence over generating solutions to another person's problem. For example, your daughter may come to you concerned because she wants to invite a friend over to the house after school and wonders how that friend will react to her brother on the autism spectrum. Your first response should be to let her talk it out while you listen carefully to find out more exactly what she worries about. If your daughter cannot come up with her own solution or is having trouble describing what worries her, or if the two of you need to come up with a joint solution, that activity can wait until she has had a chance to talk it through. Don't rush to the end (the solution) until you have explored the middle (the exact nature of her concerns). Again, the first step in effective communication with your child is to listen well. This takes practice.

Listening well is not limited to hearing words. Sometimes our behavior, gestures, and facial expressions speak a great deal to others if they are watching us closely. As a parent, you need to be attuned to what your child does not say as well as what she does say. You also need to watch her body language for more subtle clues to what she is feeling. Changes in behavior can be very important. The chatty child who has grown silent, the cheerful child who seems sad, or the cooperative child who becomes defiant each are communicating something with their behavior. Similarly, the young child who becomes clinging and needy, who seems to need a lot of attention, or who avoids her parents and turns away from their affection is probably saying without words that she is distressed.

Be attuned to your child's behavior as well as her words. If you find that she has grown moody, sad, sullen, or teary, you will want to explore what is going on. Her nonverbal behavior is an invitation for you to talk with her. Younger children, in particular, may respond quite well if you can make a good intuitive guess about their concerns. Even older children or teens may be ready to share their feelings if you ask respectfully and are not quick to judge them.

Rule 1: Choose the Right Place and Time

One of the essentials of attentive listening is being certain that the circumstances are right. Unless it is an emergency, it is best not to have an important discussion until you have the time to truly listen to your child. If your child wants to talk, but conditions are not right, you should be sure to set a time for sharing so she will know that you take her needs seriously. For example, if you are making dinner and are very distracted with everything you need to do to get a meal on the table, don't try to squeeze in a chat. What you should do, if at all possible, is say that you need to get dinner ready and suggest that you and your daughter take a walk together after dinner while your husband cleans up. When you say that, stop what you are doing, make eye contact, and then after dinner, keep your word!

If you want to initiate a conversation with your child, make sure you find the right time. The child who wants to go outside and play soccer with her friends is probably not going to be very receptive to talking to her parent. To minimize that problem you can ask her when she might have fifteen minutes to chat with you during the day. Talking while in the car is a great way to catch up or address issues in a casual way without the pressure of a face-to-face talk. If you need to call a family meeting, you should try to do so when everyone is going to be home. That varies from family to family, but many parents prefer the weekend, for example, right after breakfast or before dinner.

Rule 2: Incorporate Feedback and Affirmation

Another key aspect of effective communication is checking to be sure you understand what your child is saying and then letting her know that you understand. That can done by occasionally making comments such as "I think I know how you feel," or "uh huh," or "that must have been really upsetting." If you are not certain you understand what your child means, you can say something like, "I want to be sure I am following what you are saying. If I understand you, it makes you very sad when your brother can't play with you."

The process of reflecting feelings and confirming that you are listening carefully can be very helpful in building an atmosphere in which your child feels that you truly wish to understand her. Sometimes repeating her feelings back to her may help her clarify to herself what she is feeling. We have probably all had the experience of realizing that things sound different when we say them out loud than when we think them to ourselves.

It is important not to assume that you know what another person means when she speaks. Listen closely, and if you are not sure what she means, ask her to help you understand. We all use words, especially feeling words, differently. One person's "angry" may be another's

"boiling mad," and your friend's "happy" may be your "thrilled." Some people are more dramatic and expressive in their feeling language and others tend to be more modest and controlled in describing their feelings. It is not a matter of being right or wrong—it's just the normal variation among us in expressing feelings. For example, one of us (SLH) knew a mother who often used the word "tense" to talk about her feelings. When I probed her as what she meant by tense, she depicted an experience that fit my description of angry. She focused more on her physical sensations, which she experienced as tension, whereas I would have likely been more attuned to my angry thoughts. Going forward in conversation, I would not have known what she meant by "tense" if I had not asked.

Rule 3: Be Open about Your Own Feelings

Communication is a two-way street. In addition to being a good listener, it is important to share your own thoughts and feelings. That means modeling for your child honest communication and sharing information and feelings appropriate to the age of the child. We need to be able to tell other people what we like about them as well as what they do that bothers us. Many people find it easy to say the nice things and give compliments, but find it hard to communicate corrective feedback about annoying or inappropriate behavior. Other people are effective at sharing angry feelings, but find it harder to convey their love. Effective communication calls for being able to say both the good and the bad in ways that do not threaten the listener. Children need to know that they are loved and cherished; they also need to know what they do that troubles us. Sharing negative and positive emotions in a constructive way is a valuable parenting skill.

Adults often express their distress about what a child is doing by speaking harshly or angrily. This is usually based on the assumption that the child knows what she is doing and wishes to upset us. Although that is sometimes true, especially among adolescents, who tend to push the limits with their parents, frequently a child does not realize that what she is doing upsets us until we tell her so. Children often do things without being aware of their effect. The very young child who smears her pudding around on the table while saying, "Don't be messy" does not yet connect her words with her behavior. Even older children fail to reflect before they do things on impulse that are dangerous or destructive. A child often needs constructive feedback about a behavior in order to learn to control it. However, when adults vent strong anger rather than expressing more modulated concerns, it becomes hard for a child to listen and perhaps hard for her to make a change without losing face. It is best when our feedback is clear but not overwhelming to the child. You don't want to shame her; you want to teach her appropriate self-control.

Consider this scenario:

Mrs. G is upset with her eleven-year-old son. He was supposed to come straight home right after school but was a half hour late. That made Mrs. G late taking her daughter to her ABA instruction appointment. The girl became very agitated because her schedule was changed and she had to wait for her brother to get home.

Let's consider two possible scenarios. In the first scenario, Mrs. G immediately lays into her son for being late: "Your sister had a meltdown because you made us late for her appointment. Why can't you be more responsible?" This may be an honest sharing of feelings, but it is almost certain to leave everyone more upset without solving the problem. In the alternative scenario, after Mrs. G drives her daughter to her ABA lesson, she talks to her son while they sit in the waiting room. She calmly asks him why he was late. He explains that an older boy pushed his friend in the mud so he ran to get the teacher who was overseeing dismissal to tell her what had happened. The teacher asked him and his friend to go talk to the principal about what occurred. After that, he ran home as fast as he could but by then he was already late.

After listening patiently and acknowledging her son's position in the situation, she coolly expressed her own frustration. Mrs. G said that while she was proud that he had helped his friend, it created a problem for her because she did not know why he was late. She added that they needed to find a better way to handle situations like this.

Then it was time to problem solve. Mrs. G thought about what her son told her and it occurred to her that her son was now old enough to stay alone in the house for an hour while she drove her daughter to her lesson and back. She asked him if he would like to have a key to the house so that he could let himself in and get a snack while she drove his sister to her lessons. That way he could do a good deed, like he did today, and not worry that he would upset his parents and his sister. They also discussed the possibility of getting the son a cell phone and simple calling plan so he could be in touch if something like this came up again.

Rule 4: Accept Other People's Feelings

We may not always agree with one another, but it is important to respect the legitimacy of one another's feelings. If your daughter expresses anger to you about all the time you spend with her brother, it is important to be open to her feelings and validate them as normal and understandable. If you get angry and defensive or guilt-ridden and apologetic when she shares these feelings, it will probably close off the lines of communication. Do your best to stand in your child's shoes and see the world from her point of view. Listen respectfully to what she has to say. For example, you might say that you would probably feel the same way if you were in her situation. Or tell her you can imagine how much it must hurt her feelings. If you do that, it is likely that she will go on to share even more feelings with you. The more fully you hear your daughter's feelings the more likely you are to be able to help her.

Acknowledging that feelings are legitimate does not mean that it is okay for a child to act on them. Your daughter has to learn to talk about what she feels rather than to vent the emotions directly. For example, she should tell you that she is feeling jealous rather than teasing her brother. She can also learn with your help to tell her brother in clear, simple words that she is angry at him for something he has done. As we noted earlier, your son can learn to apologize for his behavior. Even after he has apologized, your daughter may feel that his punishment is not sufficient. Depending on if your child with ASD is able to understand the consequences of his actions and control his impulses, you may give him a brief time-out. Otherwise, you may need to explain to your daughter that his autism spectrum disorder makes it very hard for him to anticipate the consequences of his behavior and make what she might deem appropriate amends for it. You are working on teaching him to think before he acts, but that is a hard lesson for him to learn.

Getting Outside Help

Although many children respond well to parents' efforts at communicating, some do not. If you are unable to reach your child in spite of your best efforts, or if your child's behaviors are especially troubling, you may want to consider the help of a professional therapist. For example, a brother who consistently torments and provokes his sister with autism or who regularly disobeys family rules may need help from a professional. Similarly, a child who is chronically angry and resentful of her sibling on the spectrum or says that she wishes you would send her brother "away" (or worse) may need more help than you are able to give her. For some issues, a sibling support group led by a trained professional may be helpful in allowing older children to share with one another things they feel reluctant to say to their parents. In other situations, individual psychotherapy may be a better option.

As we said in Chapter 1, it is also important to remember that some kinds of learning problems occur more often in siblings of children on the autism spectrum than in the general population. It is possible that the problems your neurotypical child is having at school or at home may reflect these learning difficulties. If you suspect that your child has a learning problem or if a teacher has raised that question, you should get an assessment by a child psychologist, neurologist, or psychiatrist (see Chapter 1).

Family Conferences

Although many of the examples in this chapter have been about one-to-one communication between a parent and a child, it is also important to be able to talk as a family. As we saw in the case of the Svenson family that opened this chapter, it is useful to bring the entire family together to share information and problem solve when there is an issue that touches everyone's lives. This is the case whether the issue concerns the child with an autism spectrum disorder or any other member of the family. A family meeting can be called by any member of the family—parent or child. Although Carol and Roger Svenson called the family meeting we discussed earlier, a child is also free to ask for a meeting.

The family meeting should be viewed as a special time and there should be a set of rules followed regarding appropriate conduct (see Table 4-1). At these meetings, parents can share with children important information, ask their opinions about impending family decisions, or jointly make plans for family events. People can also brainstorm about solutions to family problems (Forgatch & Patterson, 1989). This was the strategy used by the Svenson family when they decided where to take a family vacation before Roger had to leave for Afghanistan. As the first step, everyone just tossed out ideas and someone wrote them down. Ideas can be seemingly impossible or very practical. Notice that the Svensons did not make fun of each other's ideas while they were generating their list. People who study this kind of search for solutions tell us that it is important not to judge any suggestion until the whole list is compiled. After the list is assembled, people discuss the options, sort

Table 4-1 | Rules for Family Meetings

1. The whole family should be present.
2. Televisions, cell phones, and other electronic devices are turned off and the telephone answering machine is turned on.
3. No company.
4. Everyone who wants to talk gets a turn to talk.
5. Everyone listens while one person talks.
6. People should do their best to share their thoughts and feelings.
7. It is not fair to make fun of someone else's thoughts and feelings.
8. If the family cannot agree, parents have the final word.

out the ones that are feasible, and vote for the one they prefer. Family brainstorming is a chance to let your imagination run wild for awhile!

Closing Comments

Communication is not something we do once in awhile. It pervades our lives. It is an on-going process that shifts and changes with the ages of the children and needs of the family. Sometimes you will do a wonderful job of communicating, and sometimes you will feel disappointed that you did not listen as well as you should have or did not share as openly as you wish you had. That's okay. We all have our stronger and weaker moments. What matters most is that the overall atmosphere in your family is one in which people do their best to understand each other's experiences and to solve problems together. Children can be very forgiving of the mistakes that parents make when they know their parents are trying hard to do the right thing. Besides, there is not a human in all of written history who did not make at least a few mistakes in the complex role of being a parent!

Parent Comments

I firmly believe that if Tommy had been born without autism my children would have had a vastly different childhood. Be that as it may, the suggestion I have for other parents is to be there for them and talk to them openly about their feelings, whether bad or good, concerning the sibling with autism. We as parents have shared all of our trials and tribulations concerning Tommy with our other children. We have encouraged them to voice their opinions when they wanted to. This in turn has made them feel a very important part of Tommy's life and has helped to ease the stress in many situations.

I believe that as long as a family is open and honest with each other, they can get through almost any situation. Tommy is the prime topic of conversation in our home and no matter how the children are feeling about him that day, they express those feelings. Sometimes the problem isn't completely resolved, but at least they know we are there to listen and try to help whenever we can.

We went through a hard time with our oldest boy, Martin, a couple of years ago when he was thirteen. Martin had always been a sunny, cheerful boy who was helpful with his younger sister, Emma, who has autism. All of a sudden Martin went from being social, cheerful, and helpful to a sad boy who spent most of his time in his room. When I would ask him what was wrong, he would just get sullen and go to his room. My wife and I were at our wit's end.

Finally, one day I sat him down and told him we had to talk. I told him his sadness was tearing me apart and I needed to do something to help him. Very reluctantly he began to admit that he had heard my wife and me fighting recently about what to do for Emma, who was having some severe behavior problems. I realized that by trying to protect Martin, we had just left him with half truths about what was going on. When we sat down as a family and talked, it seemed to help him a lot. My wife and I also realized how much the situation was bothering us and that we had to do something to resolve it. We ended up going for some counseling with a psychologist, who helped us a lot.

I have had many problems with my older boy. He seems to have resented his sister since the day we brought her home. When we found out she had autism and needed a lot of special care, things went from bad to worse. Then, my husband left me a few years ago, and my son has just never gotten over that. I went to a psychologist, and my son and I had some family sessions together. That has helped some. I have learned to be more honest with him and he has expressed some of his feelings. I also learned how to set more limits for him, so he has to toe the line better now. All that helps, but it is not easy and some days I feel like I am climbing up a mountain too high to walk alone.

I grew up in a family where people didn't talk very much about their feelings. I promised myself it would be different in my own family, and it is. We talk to the kids a lot about what Christopher needs to cope with his autism and we share our feelings. I think it has made a big difference all around.

5 The Balancing Act
Meeting Everyone's Needs, Including Your Own

The Patel Family

Abha Patel was weary. Since her husband died more than a year ago, she had been getting up at five o'clock each morning to do laundry, make lunches, wake the kids, make them breakfast, and get them out of the house on time to catch the school bus. When her husband, Adit, had been alive, they had shared these tasks, but now it all rested on her shoulders. It was a heavy load.

Abha had three children. Elina was her only daughter. She was ten years old and did her best to be helpful to her mother, but she was still a child, and Abha did not want to make too many demands on her. Jalad, her older son was seven and a good boy as well, but he needed a lot of help and supervision to get organized each morning and he needed reminders when he got home about doing the few simple chores that were assigned to him. Little Dev was four years old and had a diagnosis of autism spectrum disorder. Abha worked during the day while Dev was in his special preschool class, got home just before he did, and then spent a great deal of time carrying out teaching programs sent home by the school. Dev was making good progress, but the demands on Abha's time were relentless. Sometimes Jalad and Elina were clearly upset by how much attention she spent on Dev.

Abha and Adit had been devastated when they heard that Dev appeared to be on the autism spectrum. They wept together and comforted one another. Then they resolved to do all they could to help Dev, who was only eighteen months old when they got the diagnosis. The team who diagnosed Dev helped the family find a very good early intervention program that used ABA methods and Abha stayed home with Dev so that she could work with him under their guidance. Shortly after Dev turned three and his school district had placed him in a special class for preschool aged children with ASD, there came the devastating loss of Abha's husband in a car accident. The family mourned Adit's death and his absence left a big empty place in each of their lives. Dev was too young to fully understand that his father was gone and continued to look for him for some months after the funeral. It always broke Abha's heart to see him do this.

Abha was now alone with three young children who needed her. The demands of her already busy life were much more intense than ever before. Fortunately, others stepped forward to help her. Her in-laws, who adored the children, often took Elina and Jalad for the weekend so that Abha could focus more of her time on Dev. Her own parents came twice a year from India and stayed for two months each time they came. That, too, was a big help for her and for the children.

But even with the loving support of her parents and her in-laws, the role of raising three children as a single mother was daunting and Abha often worried about whether she was doing enough to meet the needs of her family. She also still deeply missed Adit, who had been the love of her life for the years they were together. In the last few months, to her surprise, she had started to wonder if there would ever be another man in her life. But her life was so busy she doubted she could even meet anyone new, much less get married again. Hardest of all, it was still her memories of Adit that filled her heart.

Introduction

Every family with children is busy. It's a fact of life for parents raising neurotypical children and even more so for those families that include one or more children with an ASD. Still more demanding is the situation that Abha faces, being a single parent with three young children, one of whom is on the autism spectrum.

Life in families with children is always a balancing act. The children need care, one's aging parents may need care; in many families, the adult partners may be frustrated by the lack of time they have to spend with one another, and parents often have little time for themselves as individuals. There is a lot of joy in the lives of many families, including those raising a child on the spectrum, but family life can also be very rigorous.

Parents make countless choices each day about where to best spend their time and energy. In some families, where both parents work to support the family, one parent may have to quit his or her job to attend to the needs of the child on the spectrum. Although that person is often the mother, in a number of families, it is the father, perhaps for reasons pertaining to temperament, earning potential, or both. Either way, family income is decreased and they may have to make significant family sacrifices to adapt to having less money.

Research suggests that mothers spend more time with a child with disabilities than with their typically developing child(ren) (McHale & V. Harris, 1992). This difference in attention can lead to jealousy and resentment from the other children in the family. As children grow up, they begin to understand why their parents have been more attentive to the child on the spectrum, but for young children, this disparity can create a fair amount of distress. It is probably not simply the amount of time spent with the child with the disability that makes the most difference to other children in the family, but what they believe this difference means. If the typically developing children feel that their parents love the child with ASD more than themselves, that will probably have a more negative impact than if they are able to understand the reason for the difference in attention. This situation is an excellent example of the importance of good communication in a family.

Abha found herself in the position of breadwinner, parent, and lone adult in her household. Except in families with exceptionally high incomes, who can afford to hire outside help, these circumstances can diminish the quality of life for the family in some respects. These challenges are further compounded by the added costs that go along with raising a child on the spectrum. Even something routine like hiring a babysitter can be more expensive when one of the children has an ASD and may require more attention than other children.

There are no perfect choices for Abha Patel and her children, just as there are no perfect solutions to the demands on any parent for time and resources. Life often involves compromise. You may sometimes make decisions that disappoint someone in your family, possibly yourself. That happens in every family, regardless of whether it includes a person with an autism spectrum disorder or not. However, if you consider your options and think about how best to address a particular situation, you will, over time, probably make many more good choices than poor ones. In addition, if you work at having good communication within your family, there will be opportunities to discuss your decisions and help your children better understand when things do not turn out as they had hoped.

You Love Him More

As a parent (or a former child), you know that children are very alert to differences in the way they are treated. Many of these differences are based on age. Older children have more freedom and more privileges than younger children. Younger children, who have fewer skills, typically get more attention than their older siblings, who have many more resources available to them. Older children usually stay up later, get bigger allowances, and have more privileges than their younger brothers or sisters do. The logic behind these decisions is clear to the parents who make these decisions but may seem unfair to the younger child who yearns for more equality. However, your child can be helped to understand that some privileges are granted not because one child is loved more than the other, but because with age comes increasing freedom as well as increasing responsibility. Even though they may protest a bit, children can usually understand the justice in this formula as long as they find

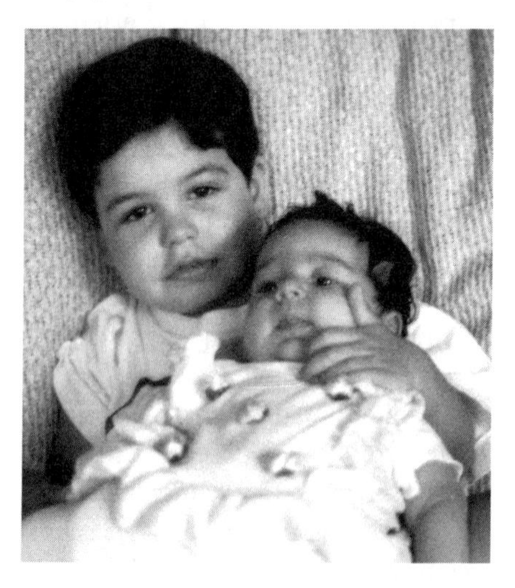

that they too receive their fair share as they grow up, and as long as they feel loved and valued by their parents.

When age is not a factor in differential treatment, it may be harder for children to grasp why their sibling is getting more parental attention than they do. This is often the situation when families include a child who has an autism spectrum disorder. Jalal and Elina watched with some resentment when they saw how much more attention Dev was getting than they were. Abha knew that Dev needed much more teaching time than her older children, but she was aware that her older children were sometimes jealous. She often felt guilty about what she was not doing for her two older children. She loved them both dearly, but feared for Dev's future.

In every family, but especially in a single parent family, this is not a simple problem to solve. We will discuss in this chapter some strategies to help each of the children in your family feel equally loved by you.

Together or Apart?

How do you feel about doing things as a family? Some parents feel strongly that all of their children should be involved in every family activity. When they go to the museum, everyone goes. When they go on a picnic, everyone goes. If they go to one child's soccer game, the whole family goes to cheer him on. When there is a child with an autism spectrum disorder parents may feel especially strongly that he should be part of family events. They want to expose their child on the spectrum to all of the things that occur in a community and they want to make it clear to the community that he is an equal member of their family. They never want to leave him out.

We understand and respect that value, but we also think there may be times when it is important to be flexible about who should attend a particular event. If your daughter has a dance recital and your son with an ASD cannot sit quietly through the performance, it may be easier on all concerned if he stays home with a babysitter while you and your spouse beam with pleasure at your daughter's performance. If your son begins to act up by making noises or flapping his hands and has to leave the room, it may be very upsetting to your young dancer when she sees one of her parents walking him up the aisle and out as she is about to perform. There are times in life when each of us needs a chance to shine in the eyes of our parents and it might be very painful for your daughter if your son's behavior deprives her of that moment.

In general, we think it is important for each child in a family to have some special time with each parent and some time with both parents. That is not, in our view, limited only to families where there is a child on the autism spectrum. Rather, it is true for every family that has two or more children. We hope you have your own fond memories of those times in your childhood when you were the focus of your parents' attention. You will want to give your own children memories like that for the years ahead.

Children on the autism spectrum require much more parental time than do neurotypical children. We realize it may not be possible to devote as much time to your typically developing children as you do to your child on the spectrum. Total equity is not the goal. The goal is ensuring that each of your children has some high quality time with each parent and with both parents. The private time need not be lengthy, or occur every day, or revolve around a special event. But your child should know that at least a few times a week, he will be able to spend some special time with his mother or father. During that time, the parent should be attentive to the child and listen carefully to him. This time may occur when a child is being tucked into bed, on a Saturday morning drive to the dry cleaners, or on a walk or jog together. For example, Abha decided she would invite her daughter to go grocery shopping with her. On the drive over and on the way back she listened carefully to Elina and responded to her concerns. She also asked Jalal to ride with her to pick up the dry cleaning and get gas for the car. Abha's in-laws had been wonderful about spending time with Elina and Jalal, but she decided to ask them to take on the somewhat more challenging task of looking after Dev on Saturday evenings so she could take Elina and Jalal out to dinner. Although she had some concerns about how well her in-laws could manage him, she found that things went fairly well as they got to know Dev better. It was a win-win situation.

Bedtime also became a nice opportunity to spend a few minutes alone with each child. Dev went to bed first and slept well, so that was easy. Jalal went to bed a little while later and Abha spent a few minutes each night talking about his day and about what he would be doing in school the next day. As the oldest child, Elina was the last child she tucked in. Before she turned off the light, Abha would ask her daughter about her day, sometimes they sang a song together, and sometimes

Elina would share a concern she had about school or home. Abha knew it would have been easier if Adit were still alive, but she was pleased to find that she could create a schedule that allowed her to be attentive to all three of her children.

A few months later Abha realized there was one person whom she was neglecting with her new schedule: herself. So, once again turning to her in-laws she asked them if they would be willing to come to her home once a month while she spent some time with friends from work or with some of the couples that she and Adit had enjoyed when he was alive. That worked so well she asked her sister and brother-in-law to also come one evening a month. It was good for her to have some time for herself. Knowing that she had a couple of evenings a month that were all hers made the daily routines easier.

If Abha did not have family members so close by she might have had to turn to other resources to get some respite. Places of worship often bring people together to share resources. Because she was raised in the Hindu religion she might have sought help from the members of her Hindu temple. People who belong to other faith groups could seek similar help from their church, synagogue, or mosque. Parents can also request respite services from state or private agencies that meet the needs of families of children on the autism spectrum. Some people place ads in a campus newspaper at a university or community college to hire caring undergraduates to come to their home and work with their child on the spectrum. Please see the section on "Using Resources" for more discussion of this topic later in this chapter.

Being Together

It is very important for every child to feel special in the eyes of his parents. It is also important to be part of a family and to do things together as a family. Being a family means, among other things, sharing time and activities together, sharing family jokes, reminiscing about family events, and planning fun activities together. It is important for your typically developing children to grow up knowing that his or her sibling on the spectrum is very much a part of the family's good times, just as they need to understand that sometimes they will do things separately from their sibling with ASD.

Avoiding Embarrassment

As they enter preadolescence, many young people become acutely concerned about how they are viewed by their peers. This is the age when many youngsters decline to walk next to their parents for fear they will not "look cool" to their classmates. Your neurotypical child may feel considerable embarrassment if his sibling with an autism spectrum disorder "acts up" in public or even if he doesn't. Some preadolescents voice these feelings directly and others start to find reasons to avoid family outings. It is important to listen respectfully to these feelings and understand that this is your child's current experience in life. It does not mean he should never have to be with his brother, but rather that some compromises may be necessary.

This sense of discomfort is not unique to youngsters who have a sibling with an ASD. Many preteens and teenagers want to "disown" their families and have strict rules for their parents about not hugging them in public, tousling their hair, or using a family nickname. Any of those and countless other infractions can earn a withering glare from a teen. Parents of young adolescents may agree not to bring a sibling with autism to an event that is important to the teen. They may also plan family activities such as riding bikes in the country or camping in a national park that do not require very much public exposure for the sensitive adolescent. These kinds of activities will let you enjoy shared times and allow your teen to relax and enjoy his family.

Your child on the spectrum may be puzzled by why his brother is ignoring him when you are on a family outing in public. But remember, family life is always a balancing act and as a parent you need to decide which things you can ignore and which require a response from you. Pick your battles wisely!

Choosing the Right Activities

Finding activities that can be shared by your child with an ASD can sometimes be a challenge. Perhaps it is helpful to understand that the skills necessary for this kind of sharing can be mastered over time, just as other skills, such as speech or self-help skills, are gradually learned and made more complex. Your child's teacher can be a valuable consultant in identifying activities within your child's abilities and in helping create programs to enable your child to learn the skills.

Examples of shared family activities that can be performed very competently by many people on the spectrum are jogging with a parent or sibling, bowling, or riding a bike. Being able to shop in a mall, participate in making a meal, or going to a movie are other activities that he can share with his family. When camping, he can learn to find small sticks for a campfire, hand his parents the pegs that hold the tent in place, and unroll his own sleeping bag. As he gets bigger and stronger he can contribute more to setting up camp and putting together snacks and meals. He can also carry his own small backpack from very early and will gradually develop the strength to carry a heavier load as he grows up. We know a young man with some very good skills who enjoys taking road trips with his family. He has learned how to read a map and reads aloud from the guidebook about points of interest as they approach those locations. This role keeps him busy and makes him an integral part of family trips.

Your child with an ASD may not learn recreational skills as quickly as his siblings, but these skills, like all the others he needs to learn, can be systematically taught and built one upon the other. Keep the individual goals modest, and gradually work toward more complex skills. If you start teaching him to jog by running just a very short distance and gradually increase it each day, he can soon be running a couple of miles very skillfully. One of our former students, now an adult, runs with his father every morning. It is a source of pleasure for both of them.

Some activities, like shopping in a mall, may be initially overwhelming for a person on the spectrum. All of the visual and auditory stimulation may make him anxious and upset. When this is the case, you need to start with very brief visits to the mall and very slowly increase the duration. You should also go during relatively quiet times of the day when there will be less activity. If you have some serious shopping to do, you should probably come in two cars. After a few minutes inside the mall your son may show some slight signs of distress. This might be thirty seconds or it might be five minutes. Whatever the duration, it is time for one person to leave and take him home while the other person continues shopping. You have averted a meltdown by being alert to your child's comfort level and the next time you may be able to increase the length of visit, if only by another small interval. Eventually, your child with autism may be able to tolerate a full trip and even enjoy the experience!

Many communities now have special movie showings or live theater presentations that are targeted for children on the spectrum and their families. These special events allow the children to talk and walk in the aisles. They also allow families to bring their own snacks so if your child is on a special diet you can bring what he needs. In addition, they typically dim, but do not turn off, the lights so that the child can still see his surroundings. It is a nice way for a family to share a movie or a children's play.

Your child may resist any new experience and want to avoid changes, but it is nonetheless important for parents to persist in introducing new things to do. If your child is to function well as an adult, he needs to learn to tolerate change, and the accompanying stress, while he is young. One of the helpful things you can do to prepare your child for a new experience is to use an activity schedule. For young children, this is typically a set of pictures showing what will happen when you go to the mall, for example. You might have a picture of your child sitting in the car, then another of the parking lot, of the building, and of walking into the mall, and so forth. For an older child, the activity schedule might consist of a set of phrases he can read that walk him through what to expect. Psychologists Lynn McClannahan and Patricia Krantz have written a very helpful book on how to use activity schedules to teach a broad array of new skills to children on the autism spectrum, *Activity Schedules for Children with Autism: Teaching Independent Behavior* (McClannahan & Krantz, 2010). Social stories and other techniques are described in *Reaching Out, Joining In: Teaching Social Skills to Young Children with Autism* (Weiss & Harris, 2001).

Private Space

Be careful not to underestimate the value of having private time for every member of your family. You may recall with pleasure the time you spent as a child stretched out on the grass watching the clouds float overhead. You may also treasure memories of working on a favorite hobby, enjoying a good book, or taking a walk by yourself. Those moments are important for children. They are also important for adults. Private time is not easy to come by in a family with young children but is still important. Time by yourself or shared with a partner or good friend is the time when you can relax and refuel, emotionally. This is not an issue of self-indulgence; it is a matter of sustaining good mental health. Although there are cultural differences in how much private time people expect, in most western families it is quite common that each parent regularly enjoys some time alone and that private time is shared between couples too. Time with your partner helps strengthen your bond as well as communicates your love for one another and ensures you have time to resolve issues that are of concern. Keeping a marriage healthy goes a long way toward giving you both the energy you need to care for your children.

Your neurotypical children also benefit from time on their own—time to ride their bikes, read a book, build a model plane, practice a dance routine, or just daydream. To ensure that they have that time means parents need to keep track of how much responsibility they ask their children to assume. Having a sibling with autism may make private time a little harder to come by so parents should ensure that childcare and household chores, along with homework, do not become so extensive that their neurotypical children have no time for themselves.

We are both committed to the idea that even young children should have some simple ways in which they contribute to the family's welfare. That might start with carrying their dish from the table to the counter, and progress to setting the table and loading the dishwasher. Especially for older siblings, it should also include spending some time with their brother or sister with an ASD. There are times of the day when asking your neurotypical child to do a relatively short stint of childcare can be especially valuable. One example is in the hour or so before dinner when the person doing the meal preparation would like to focus on that activity. That might be a good time for a brother or sister to spend time with a sibling on the spectrum. However, some children are so very helpful that their parents come to depend on them for fairly extensive childcare and that may eventually result in the older child or teen having little time to himself. Those children are in danger of giving away their own childhood.

In the description of the Patel family that opened this chapter it was clear that Abha was very concerned that she not make too many demands on her two older children to care for Dev and that she give them the attention they needed. She was especially careful not to ask too much of Elina, even though her daughter was always willing to be of help. Striking a good balance was more challenging for Abha as a single parent than it is for families in which two people share the responsibilities.

Part of protecting the rights of your typically developing children is making sure they have some private space for their possessions. Optimally, this would mean that each child would have a room of his own, with a lock on the door if necessary to ensure they can keep their belongings safe from their brother or sister with ASD. This is not always a feasible solution. If your children have to share a bedroom, you should make sure that there is a secure space where your neurotypical child can store the things he values most. That could be a locked footlocker or a designated drawer or closet. If your child with ASD frequently intrudes on his sibling's activities or tries to join in when he has friends over, you should similarly try to provide your neurotypical child with a separate space and direct your child with ASD to a different activity in another part of the house.

In spite of your best efforts to protect your neurotypical child's privacy, space, and belongings, it is likely that things will get broken or lost from time to time when your child with ASD handles them. When that happens, it is important that you express empathy for your neurotypical child's loss and, if it is possible, replace or repair the broken item. Your expression of concern and your comfort will mean a great deal to your typically developing child. You should listen attentively and let him know that you realize it is hard to have something broken that is important to him. Imposing a consequence on your child with an ASD is also appropriate in some cases. That can range from having to clean up the mess he made, to having to spend some time alone in his room (time out), to having some money taken from his allowance to help replace the broken item. These consequences have to be tailored to the age and understanding of the child with ASD.

Everyone Contributes to a Family

We have focused a great deal in this book on protecting neurotypical children from becoming auxiliary parents. Children should not have extensive childcare responsibilities after school or on weekends, nor should they be expected to be responsible for disciplining the child with ASD as an adult would. The neurotypical child might give mild reprimands such as "stop tearing up the paper," or suggest alternative games, such as "Why don't you do a puzzle now?" However, they should not be expected to require the child with ASD to clean up a mess or put the child in time out. They are also not responsible for making decisions about the welfare of their brother or sister with ASD.

Because children are not adults, they should be buffered from many of the responsibilities that fall to parents. However, they are members of the family and can assume more modest roles with their sibling on the spectrum. For example, an adolescent sibling might babysit his younger brother with ASD one evening a week or on a weekend.

A younger child can be taught how to engage his brother in play and spend some time in playful interaction each day.

Your child with ASD should also learn how to contribute to the family. Just as he can learn to share recreational activities with the family, so too can he learn how to do basic chores such as putting paper into a recycling bin, helping to rake leaves, helping plant flowers in the spring, being an assistant to the cook at mealtime, and so forth. Those skills may take years to learn, but by the time he is a young adult he will have many of the skills he needs for independent living. Photographic activity schedules, written schedules, and video models of how to complete self-help and life independence activities will be valuable tools in teaching him how to accomplish these goals (McClannahan & Krantz, 2010). For example, he could learn by following a set of photographs how to open the dishwasher, remove the clean dishes, and put them on the shelves and in the drawers where they belong. For some children, self-modeling with a video may provide a helpful model of performing a skill (Buggey, 2009). In addition to his acquiring these skills over time, your other children are less likely to resent him if he has chores of his own to do each day.

Using Resources

Perhaps as you have been reading this chapter you have wondered how it is possible for a person to do all the things we have described. Being able to spend time with each child, with your spouse, and by yourself can take a lot of juggling. You may need to draw on resources outside of your own home so that you can make time to do the things you want to do with your family and for yourself. There are two kinds of support networks to which parents can turn. One of these is their informal network of family and friends; the other is the formal network of professionals including teachers, physicians, speech therapists, and others who work with your child with ASD.

Informal Support

Although you might never have used the term, you are probably enjoying the benefits of some informal supports right now. When a friend takes your neurotypical child to his piano lesson or your mother stays with the children for a night so you can get away with your partner, those are informal supports. Informal supports are the kinds of things your family, friends, members of your faith group (church, mosque, synagogue, or temple), or people in the wider community do to help you with the problems you face in raising your child with ASD. If these good people are going to stay with your child with ASD, you will have to teach them the basics of understanding his needs so everyone is comfortable with the arrangement. The best way to do this is probably to have them come to your home a couple of times to meet your child. The first time you could show them how you interact with your son and the second time they could try to care for him with your coaching. They don't have to be experts in applied behavior analysis, but they do need to have enough of basic understanding to keep your child safe while you are away.

Very good sources of informal support in a time of crisis or if you want to get away for a couple of days are friends who also have a child on the spectrum. Although their child may be quite different from your own, that family is likely to have a pretty good set of skills for meeting the needs of children with ASD. You can arrange to "trade" childcare. That means sometimes you will take care of their daughter with ASD and they will reciprocate by doing the same with your son at a different time. It will be hectic when you have both children, but quite lovely when they have both youngsters! Plus, your houses are probably already "child proofed" so no preparations are needed when you swap overnight stays!

As we have suggested in this book, your family's mental health is at stake, so you should not be shy about asking other people to lend a hand. It makes other people feel good when they can help you and it gives you a chance to have some relief from the rigor of most of your days. Engaging other people in your life helps to build a broad sense of community. We both think that the notions of self-sufficiency and rugged individualism have little benefit for families of children with ASD. Although various cultures around the world have adhered to those values at different times in their histories, living by those principles tends to undermine a sense of connection with one's community. Our own experience is that when we are allowed to give to others, it enhances a sense of community and common ground. So, calling on your relatives and friends is not just good for your own family, but also for the contribution it makes to the welfare of the people who become your supports.

Research on informal support networks suggests that the wider your support network, the stronger and more effective it will be. That makes good sense. If there were only two people you could count on, they might move, get tired of being called on so often, or get older and not have the energy needed to keep up with your children. But, if you have many people in your social support network, you can call on each individual less often and if someone can't help there is always a backup person who can help. Having a good network of caring people will reduce your vulnerability to sadness and feelings of isolation. Even if your mother or mother-in-law tells you that she wants to do it all, it is essential that you build a wide network that ensures you will have support when you need it. This approach also gives the neurotypical children in your family other adults to whom they can turn if they need help.

Although family members are often wonderful sources of support, they may not always fully understand the extent of the demands that you face. Some years back we did a study comparing how parents of a child with ASD and the grandparents of that child viewed the impact of the child's special needs on the family (Harris, Handleman, & Palmer, 1985). Perhaps because they do not usually live with the child, the grandparents may not fully comprehend how much of a challenge the child's needs pose to the family's life. It may also be that parents do not fully share with their own parents the extent of the impact of the child on their own lives. They may not want to upset their parents or may feel that their stress is an issue to remain within their own nuclear family and not be discussed with parents or other relatives. This is not unlike the reluctance of some adolescents to disclose to their parents some of their own concerns about things like whether they could transmit the genes that cause ASD to their own children or what their parents expect from them should they become responsible for their adult sibling on the spectrum. Just as your children want to protect you, you too may be trying to protect your own parents. However, parents who have shared some of their concerns with their own parents tell us that these grandparents are likely to become one of their most important sources of support.

Be sure to tell your extended family what you need from them as well. If Uncle Zack and Aunt Bess invite your family to their annual cookout, you need to tell them how they can create conditions that make it possible for you to come. For example, if all of the noise and movement of the whole family is upsetting to your child on the spectrum, you can discuss some of the options. One would be that you stop by for just a short visit and leave before your child has a meltdown. Another would be that they set aside a room in the house where your daughter with ASD can stay and that some of the family members whom she knows would visit one at a time. Alternatively, if none of these ideas are feasible, it may be easier for your family to stay home and have cookout of your own. Your relatives will not know what your child needs until you tell them, and once they understand, most people will go out of their way to accommodate your whole family. If your child on the spectrum is comfortable, then your other children will be also.

Formal Support

Your pediatrician, children's dentist, speech therapist, teachers, behavior analyst, and other professionals who work with you and your child are all part of your formal support network. These are the professionals in your community who provide essential services to people with ASD. For example, some agencies provide respite care for families who need emergency help or wish to take a weekend off from childcare. In-home respite care involves having a trained person come into your home to provide care for your child with ASD. Alternatively, out-of-home respite means that the child has a short-term placement in the home of a respite worker or in a group home that provides short-term respite placements and may also offer long-term placements for some clients who cannot remain at home. Out-of-home respite might be a good option if you or someone else in the family needs to have surgery and will require some quiet time to recover after the procedure.

Some people are shy about asking for respite care. We think you should ask for every resource that is potentially useful to you. People who are chronically exhausted often can't provide the quality of care that their children need. They would be much more effective if they were rested and able to bring all of their energy to their work. Your local Autism Society of America chapter, ARC, or Easter Seals program may be able to help you find agencies that provide respite care in your area. Respite services may be paid for by your state or county government, but you will have to register with the state to receive these benefits. Unless your family is in an emergency situation, there is typically a waiting list for these services. So it is a good idea to be proactive and register early in order to gain some priority over time.

Parent Support Groups

Parent support groups have the potential to offer several benefits to you as an individual and to your family as a whole. One of these benefits is the opportunity to share your feelings and concerns with other parents who face similar difficulties. It can be comforting to realize the extent to which other people share your concerns. It can also be very helpful to hear how they have solved problems that you have not been able to address successfully. Other people's solutions may give you ideas about how to solve the problems that you and your family face. As we mentioned earlier in this chapter, other parents may also be able to provide tangible help, such as short-term childcare, joining together to take all of the children on an outing, sharing childcare, or providing the name of a pediatrician who is attuned to the needs of children with ASD. Over the years, both of us have had the privilege of leading parent support groups and have witnessed first-hand how valuable these exchanges among parents can be.

Parent support groups discuss a wide range of topics. One topic raised fairly often is the sense of "guilt" about their inability to meet the needs of their typically developing children as well as their child on the spectrum. Parents also talk about how to explain autism spectrum disorders to their neurotypical children as well as how to explain it to a high functioning child on the spectrum, who often feels very lonely and left out of the social groups that other children form. Many parents discuss wanting to have another child, but worry about conceiving another child with ASD. If you want a forum for talking about these kinds of topics and hearing how other people cope with similar challenges, a parent support group may be a very good option. These are people who are "walking the same walk" as you and your family and therefore have a good understanding of what you are going through. Some treatment programs and schools for children with ASD and some community organizations offer parents support groups. Your child's teacher, the local chapter of the Autism Society of America, or another statewide autism advocacy agency may be able to help you find a group that meets close to where you live.

If you live in an isolated area where there are few other families who have a child on the spectrum or prefer not to converse face-to-face with others, you may find it helpful to join an online conversation (i.e., chat room, listserv) for families with children with ASD. The website addresses of these groups often change and your best bet is to do a search for "online support groups for parents of children with autism," as there are many that are available and they serve a variety of families with special interests.

We do want to offer you some words of caution. Most family support chat rooms will have a mix of communications. Some of them offer wisdom and some of them may focus more on myth. You need to be an informed consumer because people are free to write almost anything they wish online and some of what you find will have a good research base and some will be deceptive or fraudulent. Be careful what you accept as "truth." Neither of us regularly follows a listserv or visits a chat room so we cannot endorse a specific resource. That said, many parents tell us they enjoy the ease and anonymity of an online group and often get useful advice from other parents.

Another option for families who live in isolated areas is to make contact with other families who also live in remote places and be in touch through e-mail or a video call connection. This is a more personal and direct way to communicate and because you know the people with whom you are communicating, you are at less risk of being vulnerable to the bias of people who may promote a particular chat room. Siblings can enjoy this format for communication at least as much as their parents do. You may be living far from other people but you do not have to be alone.

Sibling Support Groups

Support groups are not limited to parents. Siblings value the experience too. Sibling groups can give children an opportunity to talk about feelings such as anger at their peers who reject their brother or sister on the autism spectrum, fear of "inheriting" the ASD genes, jealousy over the attention that their brother or sister gets from parents, and how they resent having to compete for attention from their parents. All of this and more constitute common themes in sibling support groups. Many children find that sharing their feelings with other children eases their discomfort in talking about topics that are harder to raise with their parents. Sometimes it is easier to voice these feelings outside of the family, and other children can help to affirm the acceptable nature of uncomfortable feelings. In the groups we run, we invite parents to attend the last session where the children, as a group, tell parents about the kinds of things they worry about. This presentation may make it easier for parents and children to then pursue resolution to some of these concerns at home.

Unlike parent support groups, where the participants often set the agenda for the meetings, our sibling groups have a planned sequence that extends across several weeks. The number of participants ranges from six to twelve children and when there is a broad age range we usually divide the children into older and younger subgroups according to their interest in and ability to understand various issues. For example, elementary school-aged children are not likely to be concerned about the genetics of ASD, but for teenagers this can be a very important issue.

Each meeting includes a group activity, a group discussion, and a snack time. At the first meeting, the children may make a group drawing and select a name for their group to help create a sense of connection among them. They may also talk about what kids with autism are like and this serves to help them realize there are other children who share their experiences. As the weeks progress, we discuss a broad array of age appropriate topics including individual differences among children in general and between each child and his or her sibling, problem solving skills to deal with issues that arise in their relationship with their sibling on the spectrum, how to engage a brother or sister in ASD in playful interactions, and so forth.

Another useful resource for people who wish to create sibling support groups is a book by Don Meyer and Patricia Vadsay (2008). That book was written as a guide for siblings of children with a broad array of special needs including children on the autism spectrum.

Your child's teacher or your local Autism Society of America chapter may be able to help you find a sibling support group in your community. You will want to make sure that the person who runs the group has appropriate credentials such as being a school psychologist, clinical psychologist, or social worker. Other people, unless they have been very well trained by a member of one of the helping professions, may have very good intentions but not understand how children differ developmentally as they grow up and may overlook the indications that a particular child needs help beyond what can be provided in a sibling support group. At the Douglass Developmental Disabilities Center, the sibling groups are run by doctoral students in clinical or school psychology under the close supervision of an experienced clinical psychologist. At or before the first meeting, we explain our plans for keeping the conversations in the sibling group confidential, but also tell the children that we will inform parents if there are themes emerging for their child that suggest he might benefit from professional services beyond what the group offers.

Closing Comments

Living in a family is one of the most challenging things we do. There are so many competing needs to be met, and so little time to meet them. If your child has ASD, the demands of family life may be even more intense than in other families because that child needs so much extra help to realize his potential in life. The stress created by those demands can be a breeding ground for anxiety, tension, sadness, jealousy, and other painful emotions on the part of any family member.

Meeting the many demands of family life and helping each family member develop a fulfilling life may hinge in part on your ability to draw on the resources around you. It makes good sense to ask family, friends, and professionals to contribute what they can to help your family thrive. If you are a single parent or a couple raising your children far from the support of your own parents, you may need to make an extra effort to reach out to your friends in the community. The more helpers you have, the better.

Fortunately, although family life is demanding, it can also be profoundly rewarding, and your neurotypical children may emerge as richer adults for having been part of a family that included a child with ASD.

Parents Speak

In keeping with this idea of occupying Matt's time, we have encouraged him to be independent and responsible around the house. He can cook, set the table, load the dishwasher, bring out the trash, etc. He has also developed interests in coloring, reading, arts and crafts, and helping his dad paint and work with tools on various home projects.

I sometimes think back to that powerfully energetic toddler. What I see today is an eight-year-old boy who is constructively busy most of the time, and happy being so. This has allowed me more time with my daughter, and a more relaxed and happy family life in general.

In giving direction to Matt's life, we have managed to take control of ours. When I now take some time for myself, I find it is not motivated by a desperate need, but by more of a healthy desire.

I know I am not an expert at managing the complex balancing act within our family. I hope I am doing a decent job, but sometimes I'm not so sure. Unfortunately, parents of children with autism aren't given any special graces to deal with these circumstances. We are just ordinary people in very extraordinary situations.

I really feel there is a part of your life you must neglect to keep up with the other demands. In my case, I have never worked outside the home since Tommy's problems began. Some people may be able to work, but I always felt I could not give my all to both at the same time.

It was hard for me at first, but I have finally started to ask other people for help. We applied to a local agency for respite care. We get twenty hours a month and that has made a big difference for all of us. My husband and I make it a point to go out together at least once a week, even if it is just for a movie.

One of the hardest things for me was letting my family know that I needed more help from them. My mom said I always seemed to have everything under control and she didn't want to intrude. Once I told her I could use the help, she was great.

One of the toughest things for me about my son's autism has been how my family has reacted. When my parents heard that Dick had autism they just seemed to disappear. They never offer to sit with him. My sister-in-law asked me to leave Dick at home when they had a family party and invited all the other children. Those things just go right to my heart. So, I don't see much of my family, but it hurts a lot. When we talk in our parent support group about how some people have families who are so great in helping, I just want to cry all over again.

My husband and I have been trying to get together with other parents of children with autism and do things together. Sort of make a new family to help each other. It isn't the same as if my mom did it, but it helps to have friends who care.

When our teenager was thirteen, he went through a time when he did not want to be seen in public with us. If we went to the mall, he would walk about a dozen paces behind me so that people would not see him with me and think he wasn't "cool." I can understand that. I went through it myself when I was young. What was hard for me was that he especially did not want to be seen with his younger sister who has autism.

She can be quite a handful, doing things like dropping to the floor and having a tantrum in the middle of a shopping trip. I wasn't sure if I should insist on her being with us, but I finally realized that if I pushed him very hard it might make more trouble.

He was good to his sister at home. If we were hiking in the woods or some place private, he would take care of her, but put him within fifty yards of another adolescent and it was a different story. That phase passed by the time he was fifteen, and now he seems very comfortable with us and with her. As I look back, I'm glad his mother and I did not push it too hard, and I'm glad we still managed to find some family things to do that were private enough for my son to be at ease. Growing from boy to young man is tough going.

ꟷ

My seven-year-old daughter who has autism broke one of her brother's favorite toys the other day. He was very upset and wanted me to punish her. At first I thought it wouldn't do any good, but then I realized that even if she didn't learn anything, my son would feel that I was standing up for him and it would make him feel better. So, I sent her to her room.

ꟷ

My daughter's development and independence are as important as my son's, therefore we try not to restrict her activities because of his challenging behaviors. For instance, I take him to her baseball games, running errands, church, etc., and work on teaching him appropriate behavior, as painful as it is for all of us!

Juggling their schedules is probably the biggest challenge, especially since neither one understands why they have to go to the other's events. Quite often my son tantrums and creates undue attention toward us, which my daughter absolutely hates.

ꟷ

6 Children at Play
Helping Children Play Together

The Jackson Family

Seven-year-old Emily Jackson ran to her mother with tears streaming down her face. "She hates me, Mommy. She hates me. When I wanna plays she just looks the other way. She hates me." Sharon Jackson knelt down to hug her daughter and help her regain her composure. She soothed and held Emily until she was calm and then dried her tears. "She doesn't hate you, Sweetie, she just doesn't know how to play."

The "she" in question is Emily's five-year-old sister, Cheryl, who has a diagnosis on the autism spectrum. Although she has some limited speech, makes fleeting eye contact, can imitate the motor actions of her teacher, and follow simple directions, she shows little interest in her sister. Emily, by contrast, really wants to play with her sister and repeatedly tries to tempt her with toys. Usually, Cheryl just turns her back on her sister or flaps her hands in front of her face, but if Emily persists, she might begin to scream and rock.

Later that evening, after both children are asleep, Sharon and her husband, Jessie, talk about what had happened during the day and Sharon describes how upset Emily had been when Cheryl ignored her efforts to play. Jessie, who is a much loved science teacher and track coach at the local high school, explains that he had been talking to his coworker, Beth, that day and that Beth had told him about a support group for siblings of children on the spectrum that was being offered at a nearby university. Beth said one of the things they did for the children was teach them how to engage their sibling in play. Beth had sent her neurotypical son their last year and he learned a lot of useful things he could do to get closer to his sister on the spectrum. He enjoyed it so much he wanted to go back again this year.

Sharon liked the idea of the sibling group and called the university the next day for information about the support group. She found out that a new group was going to start in three weeks and they had an opening in their youngest group for children seven to ten years of age. They only charged three dollars a week to cover the cost of snacks and art materials.

When Jessie arrived with Emily for the first group session he walked her into the building to make sure she knew where to go. He looked around with delight at the children who were there for the meeting who seemed to come from a wide range of racial and ethnic groups. He was heartened to know that Emily, who is African-American, would feel very much at ease with the blend of children in the group.

Sharon picked Emily up after the first meeting and Emily was very excited. "Mommy, guess what? They all have a brother or sister like Cheryl. Can you believe it? Every single one of the kids is just like me. Wow! We are going to do lots of really cool stuff and they are even going to teach me how to play with Cheryl."

A few weeks later, when Emily came home from the group, she told her parents she was going to be Cheryl's teacher. She collected some of the farm animals Cheryl had in her room and the little plastic barn where the animals lived. She also got a cookie from the kitchen and broke it into tiny pieces so she could use it as a reward for Cheryl when she did what she asked her to do. She knew she would have to start slowly with Cheryl or she would ignore her, so for her first "lesson" she just showed Cheryl the horse and said, "Look Cheryl, it's a horse." If Cheryl glanced at it Emily gave her a bit of cookie and said, "Great job, Cheryl!" or "You looked at the horse!" Her voice was full of delight when she looked and she smiled at Cheryl a lot and patted her on the back. After about five minutes of showing her various animals and praising her for looking, Emily said to Cheryl, "See you later," and she gathered up the toys and left her to do what she wanted. Later in the day Emily did the same routine again and Cheryl seemed interested in listening to her. She thought Cheryl might find the cookie a very nice reward for listening to her.

Over the course of the next few weeks, Emily gradually increased her demands on Cheryl. For example, she'd say to her, "I am going to put the cow in the barn," and walk the cow to the barn. Then she'd ask Cheryl, "Now you put the pig in the barn," and when she made no attempt to do so, she'd put her hand on the pig and guide Cheryl to put the pig in the barn, praising her for doing so. She gradually reduced her physical prompts and Cheryl was soon walking all of the animals into the barn. Next she'd ask Cheryl, "What does the horse say?" Cheryl knew the answer to that because her parents read her books about animals. So she'd say "neigh" and Emily would give her a big high five and say "What a smart girl you are!"

The more they played together, the more fun it became for both children. Eventually, Emily could ask Cheryl what game she wanted to play and Cheryl would go get the toys they needed. A couple of times Cheryl even brought some toys to Emily without her asking if she wanted to play.

Introduction

Emily's frustration at not being able to play with her sister is not unusual for siblings of children on the spectrum. Neither is the pleasure she felt once she mastered some basic skills and was able to engage Cheryl in simple play activities. Our own work with young siblings has shown us time and again that these youngsters are delighted to have the tools they need to communicate and interact with their brothers or sisters. Moreover, there are research data showing that both children are happier after they are able to interact with one another. We will discuss that research in greater depth later in this chapter.

If you think that these basic play skills may be helpful for your children, you should find a lot of useful information in the next few pages. We will briefly describe how siblings can help their brother or sister on the spectrum learn to play. We will also discuss some of the dilemmas that parents face when they ask their child to be a "teacher" and how to try to ensure that your child really wants to take on the task. Then we will describe in some detail how one of our colleagues, David Celiberti, developed and evaluated a series of steps for teaching young children to engage their brother or sister with a spectrum disorder in play. It is important to remember that the ages of each of your children and the degree of intellectual disability shown by your child on the spectrum are important factors in how complex the play interactions are likely to become.

Children as Teachers

A study by psychologists Nabil El-Ghoroury and Raymond Romanczyk (1999) looked at how parents and siblings play with a child who has an ASD. They found that parents tried harder to engage their child with an ASD in playing than they did to engage their neurotypical child. The more impaired the child's functioning was, the more effort parents put into trying to support her play. This effort on the part of the adults appears to reflect their wish to compensate as best they can for the deficits in their child's skills. In contrast, siblings made fewer efforts to help their brother or sister compensate for a lack of play skills and most made relatively few attempts to play with their brother or sister. It is encouraging to note, however, that in spite of the relative lack of effort on the part of the neurotypical siblings, the children with ASD showed some interest in mutual play.

The study by El-Ghoroury and Romanczyk suggests that if neurotypical children had the necessary skills to engage their brother or sister with ASD in some reciprocal play, the child on the spectrum might be responsive to those efforts. That interest in their typically developing sibling provides support for thinking that mutual play is possible. Happily, parents who have learned some of the basics of applied behavior analysis can teach some of the simplest of these skills to the sibling, who can use them to engage her sibling with ASD in play. We will describe below the nature of these basic teaching skills.

A study by Ferraioli and Harris (2011) demonstrated that siblings can teach their younger brother or sister on the spectrum to engage in joint attention. Joint attention (JA) occurs when one person follows the gaze of another person to see what she is looking at. We do this, for example, when we stand at the Grand Canyon, say "Wow!" and turn to see if the person we are with is also gazing in awe at the sight before us. The sharing of information through joint attention is a crucial component of effective communication. Many children on the autism spectrum are slow to develop JA and consequently may not have their gaze coordinated with a parent who looks up at the moon and says, "Look, moon." Instead, she may be looking at a tree or a streetlight. As a result, she often does not benefit from the labeling that parents do for children to teach them the names of objects.

Suzannah Ferraioli and I (SLH) taught four typically developing children, ages six to eight years of age, to encourage their siblings with ASD to engage in joint attention during play. The children on the spectrum were between three and five years of age. As a result of their interactions with their neurotypical siblings, responding to bids for JA was achieved by all four children with ASD, and three of them learned to initiate bids for JA with their neurotypical sibling. The neurotypical siblings were first taught to tap a toy to gain the attention of the sibling with ASD, then to show the toy to the child, and then to hold the toy out to the child and wait for eye contact before giving her the toy. Then the typically developing sibling made eye contact with her sister, pointed at an object, and shifted her gaze toward that object. The siblings with ASD learned to shift their gaze to the place where their brother or sister was looking. The bids for JA by the child with ASD required that child to spontaneously point at an object in the room and for the neurotypical sibling to make a very affirming response, i.e., "Wow! Great picture."

Although the study was done with young children on the autism spectrum, it is likely that it would work with older children as well. Although it has not yet been tested, it is worth trying. We hope you will let us know if your neurotypical child is able to teach the skill to an older brother or sister with an ASD.

Behavioral Techniques as Teaching Tools

Many of the parents who read this book are no doubt familiar with the basic principles of applied behavior analysis (ABA). These basic principles underlie a broad array of instructional procedures that have proven to be highly effective in teaching people of all ages on the autism spectrum. There are ABA procedures for teaching self-help skills, personal safety skills, vocational skills, educational knowledge, social skills, and communication skills. These same basic principles underlie how we teach play skills to children on the spectrum and how your neurotypical child can engage her sister with autism in playful interactions.

For those who are unfamiliar with ABA, the teaching approach involves:

- the use of rewards (positive reinforcement) such as hugs, tickles, little bits of food, or "high fives";
- well-delivered instructions that are simple and brief such as "Give me cat";
- physical, visual, and verbal guidance (prompts), such as gently guiding a child's hand toward the correct item and then removing that support as soon as possible, or saying the first sound of a word. For example, asking "What is this?" while holding up a ball and giving a verbal prompt for the initial sounds of the answer, saying "ba...." Initially, one would hold up the ball and ask "What is this?" and supply the full name, "ball" and then gradually fade the amount of help from "ball" to "ba" to "b" to silence.

There is good research evidence showing that consistency of teaching methods and expectations for the quality of responses across settings and across people is very important in helping children with ASD learn. These children seem to do their best when there is a high degree of consistency in other people's expectations for them. If a teacher at school is reinforcing (rewarding) a child with praise and access to her favorite toys for attempts to communicate, and her parents do not know they should do the same, the child will have greater difficulty learning to use her speech at home.

The use of ABA teaching methods for children on the spectrum was first tested in the mid-1960's, and by the early 1970's it was clear that for these methods to be effective, parents needed to become partners with professionals in implementing the teaching procedures (Lovaas, Koegel, Simmons & Long, 1973). Without that around the clock consistency many children on the spectrum had a great deal of difficulty transferring their skills from school to home or the community (generalizing). The effect of teaching parents the underlying principles of ABA and the specific techniques they need to use at home has helped ensure that each child is able to fulfill his or her potential. Parents who are active participants in their child's education are making a vital contribution to their child's development.

Given the valuable role of parents as teachers, it is not surprising that some people have wondered whether siblings could learn and apply behavioral teaching skills. The answer to this question is a clear "yes." A motivated child can learn the basics of ABA, and these techniques will be helpful in engaging their brother or sister in playful behavior. Children are not adults, however, and cannot assume a mature, adult role in the education of a sibling with an ASD. A neurotypical child's chronological age and level of personal maturity need to be taken into account when deciding whether to teach her techniques for playful interactions with her sibling on the spectrum. What we can expect from a seven-year-old will be different than what we can expect from a sixteen-year-old, and for any child, the expectations should be different than those we have for adults.

Furthermore, there is another important question that must also be addressed concerning the ethics of asking children to teach skills to their brother or sister with an ASD. Is it appropriate for children, especially young ones, to assume some responsibility for their siblings on the spectrum? Should they be spending an hour or two a day interacting with their brothers or sisters with ASD? Many parents have concerns about imposing too many demands on their children. You might well argue that children should be allowed to be children and not take on the role of small adults. We share those concerns. Children—even teenagers—are not adults, and should not be asked to assume the responsibilities of adults. Which brings us to the next question: If children should not be expected to take on responsibilities like managing a sibling's disruptive behavior or mastering academic, self-help, or speech skills, is there still a meaningful role they can play in the lives of their siblings with an ASD? We believe there is.

Some years back, one of us (SLH) participated in a study to determine whether young siblings of children with an ASD could use simple behavioral skills to engage their brother or sister in play (Celiberti & Harris, 1993). In doing that study we did not want to place the neurotypical sibling in the role of auxiliary parent, but rather help the children become more fully siblings. We were delighted to find that not only were siblings with ASD and neurotypical siblings capable of learning to play together, but that they had a good time doing so.

Teaching Play Skills

Psychologist and behavior analyst David Celiberti has done research on teaching siblings how to play with their brother or sister on the spectrum and he applies what he learned in these studies to his consultations with individual families (Celiberti, 1993; Celiberti & Harris, 1993). In his earliest study he worked directly with the siblings, teaching them how to use ABA skills such as praising good play, and how to initiate new games with their brother on the spectrum. However, he realized that a better way to disseminate these skills to young children would be to teach their parents how to tutor their neurotypical child in the use of basic ABA methods. That approach enabled him to keep the focus on the family as a whole. His research showed that parents can be good teachers of ABA skills. At least as important, he found that the children enjoyed playing together. In his research, Celiberti showed parents how to teach ABA skills to their child and then measured the changes in how the children played together. He found that the neurotypical children became more skillful playmates and that they enjoyed being with their brother or sister with an ASD more after training than they had before.

In teaching children how be playmates, Celiberti found it was important that the neurotypical siblings want to learn these ABA skills rather than being pressured into doing so. Celiberti talked to each child privately before the training began to ensure that the child was motivated to learn the new skills. A few children decided they did not want to be part of the project and Celiberti honored that gracefully and supportively. You will need to make a similar assessment of your own child's motivation. You should not pressure a reluctant child to learn ABA skills. Instead, explore why your child is reluctant and help her try to solve those problems. For example, your child may resent the time demands, be afraid of her sister's aggressive behavior toward her, worry that she won't be good at learning the new skills, or have some angry or jealous feelings toward her sister with ASD. Only do the training if your child truly wants to learn the skills and be sure to stop if she asks to do so.

Before you can teach your children how to play together, you yourself need to understand the basics of ABA teaching. Quite simply—you can't teach what you don't know! The skills you should know include:

- how to give clear, simple instructions,
- how to reward good behavior, and
- how to help when your child needs a prompt in order to respond.

If you have not had any training in applied behavior analysis, you may want to seek some parent training before you try to teach these skills to your children. The brief overview we are providing you in this chapter will help you understand a few of the teaching methods of ABA, but it is in the best interest of your child on the spectrum that you become fluent in these and other skills so you can teach her efficiently and effectively. Parents need a broad repertoire of skills to meet the needs of their child on the autism spectrum. There are some good books you can use to refresh your memory about teaching techniques, such as, the book *Self-Help Skills for People with Autism* by psychologist Stephen Anderson and his colleagues (2007) and a book by psychologists, Ron Leaf and John McEachin (1999), *A Work In Progress: Behavior Management Strategies and a Curriculum for Intensive Behavioral Treatment of Autism*, about using ABA techniques. People who can teach you these skills include a board certified behavior analyst (BCBA), a psychologist skilled in the use of ABA, or an educator experienced in using ABA in a school setting. In New Jersey, the state where we both live and work, there is a state-wide advocacy agency called Autism New Jersey that provides parent training groups across the entire state. Your own state or local school district may have similar resources. Ask your child's teacher, pediatrician, someone at your local ASA chapter, or the person who diagnosed your child where you might find those resources.

There are three broad steps you need to take to teach your typically developing child to become an effective teacher/playmate for his brother or sister on the autism spectrum.

1. First, remember to go slowly, do just a little each day, and be liberal in your praise of both of your children and take pride in yourself for what you are doing for them.
2. Second, create an attractive setting for teaching/play.
3. Third, teach your neurotypical child three basic skills:
   - giving instructions,
   - rewarding good behavior, and
   - prompting new skills.

Setting the Stage for Play

Before you start to teach, you should create an attractive setting for play between your children. You can maximize the likelihood of their enjoying playing together if you:

- Select activities that are age appropriate and that are likely to encourage interactions between the children rather than isolate play.
- Don't overdo the number of teaching sessions on any single day.
- Model appropriate play skills yourself.

Selecting Appropriate Activities

When selecting play activities, it is important to select toys that are colorful, attractive, and of potential interest to both children. Examples of toys that encourage interactions include such things as soft balls that can be rolled or thrown by children, trucks or cars, dollhouses, toy airports, garages, barns with animals, and doctor kits. By contrast crayons, scissors, books, and many electronic games lend themselves more readily to separate, parallel play where each child may be doing his or her own thing. For the teaching sessions you are creating, select toys that are likely to encourage joint attention from your children.

Begin with toys that are already familiar to your child with an ASD so that she understands them and knows how to manipulate them. If you are not certain that she knows how to play with a particular toy, find that out in a play session of your own. As you saw in the case of Emily and Cheryl that opened this chapter, Emily presented her sister with some of Cheryl's own toys because those were familiar to Cheryl, and Emily had seen her hold them in the past. After the children had some success with those familiar toys, Emily gradually introduced Cheryl to new toys. In the beginning, stick to familiar toys so there is good chance both children can be successful.

Toys and Activities for Younger Children. Toys should encourage interaction; they should also be age appropriate. Select toys taking into account the developmental levels of both children. Furthermore, the complexity of the toys and activities should not exceed either child's skill level. For example, a seven-year-old neurotypical brother might play "firefighters" with his younger sister on the spectrum. He would pretend to rescue a baby doll from a burning house and then guide his sister to pretend she is the doctor who takes care of the baby doll. He would give her the doctor's kit and suggest she check to see how the baby's heart sounded and to check her blood pressure. If your neurotypical child is six or younger, he might find it difficult to structure pretend play for his sibling with ASD and they might do better with more concrete play. Emily and her sister Cheryl started by moving the animals into the barn and then added making the sounds of the animals as they played.

Keep in mind the intellectual ability of your child with ASD. If she has an average IQ or higher, she will be able to master more complex play

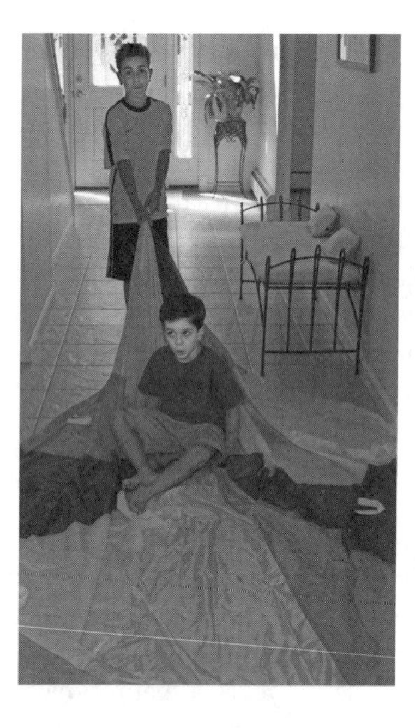

than if she has an intellectual disability (what used to be called mental retardation). Depending on the extent of her intellectual disability, she may have a hard time mastering the rules of some games or forming the concepts needed for some activities that require sorting by color, number, or shape. Her chronological age will not be a useful way to judge which games will suit her best. You should rely on her developmental age to select activities that she can master without too much distress. Your child's fine motor skills also need to be considered and you should choose materials that she can manipulate easily.

Games and Activities for Older Children. Teenagers with an ASD are too old for the kinds of play we just described. For teens, the focus should be on playing video games, ball games, age appropriate board games and card games, and learning the latest teenage dances. Preteens and teenagers can also learn to use exercise equipment, jog with a parent or sibling, or go bowling. Children of all ages can go hiking or camping with their families, and as they get older can assume greater responsibility for setting up the tent, carrying a heavier backpack, and so forth.

The focus of this chapter is on teaching young children on the spectrum to play with a neurotypical brother or sister. Nonetheless, the same ABA teaching methods that helped your neurotypical child engage her sister with an ASD when they were young can continue to be useful as they grow up. If your neurotypical child is much younger than your child with an ASD, the activities they do together will have to be appropriate for the younger child as well as the older. It is better that an activity be too easy than too hard. Your child's teacher may have some great ideas for materials that will engage the children and may be able to tell you where to shop for useful items.

Scheduling Play Sessions

Begin with very short sessions. In the very beginning, they might be just five minutes. You can gradually increase the time as the children become more comfortable with one another. A parent should be present for these initial sessions because the neurotypical child will need coaching. These early sessions are intended for teaching the children how to interact. Later, when they can play together comfortably, you may not need to be present. Eventually, your children might be having one or two play sessions a day. The children will probably enjoy the play and extend it to longer intervals even without your having to suggest that. However, if your child with an ASD poses management issues, you should be within listening distance so you can step in if she becomes aggressive toward her brother.

Modeling Play Skills

To teach your child the specific skills he will need, you should first model the behavior yourself. For example, if you are teaching your son how to get his sister's attention, start the session by sitting down with your child with ASD among the toys. Your neurotypical child should sit nearby and watch you. Show your son how you make sure his sister is physically oriented toward you and looking at you when you give a direction. If necessary, move so that you are directly facing your child and gently tilt her face toward yours. After demonstrating this for a few minutes, give your son a chance to practice the skill and praise him liberally for his attempt to do as you suggest.

Switch places with your son and do your coaching from the sideline. Give your son lots of positive feedback and gentle suggestions for improvement. For example, you could say, "That was super the way you got Alice to look at you. Don't forget to make sure she is turned toward you when you start talking." In the beginning, it will probably be your praise rather than his sister's cooperation that will sustain his effort. You daughter with ASD may be quite indifferent to her brother's attempts to engage her early on, and she won't be much of a playmate. You can sustain his effort with your praise and high-fives. Be both generous and specific with your praise. Tell him exactly what he did right. For example, "It was great the way you got her to look at the airplane." Your pleasure in his achievements should be clear from your voice and your body language.

Each time you model good teaching skills for your neurotypical child, you will need to include all of the components of good teaching, but your focus will be on one component of the procedure at a time. If you are teaching your neurotypical son to give good directions, emphasize how that is done, even though you will also be rewarding your child on the spectrum for her appropriate responses. Shine the spotlight on one skill at a time until your son is proficient in that behavior before you add the next skill. He may well begin to learn some of the other skills just by watching you and if he does, you should praise him for those actions as well, but still focus your teaching on one skill at a time.

A very important word of caution: Young children should not be expected to deal with a sibling's aggression, tantrums, or other disruptive behaviors. That is your responsibility as a parent. You should always be ready to intervene in a play session if your child with an ASD engages in dangerous behavior. If your neurotypical child is to learn to engage his sister with an ASD, it is very important that he feels safe in her presence. Some children on the spectrum may engage in a flurry of disruptive behavior in the first few sessions while their neurotypical sibling is learning to be a good teacher/playmate because the sessions themselves have not yet become reinforcing. Be sure you keep those behaviors under good control and gradually fade yourself out of the play sessions until you can be in a different room.

Giving Clear Instructions

Being a good teacher involves knowing how to give instructions. The first step to teach your child in giving an instruction is to make sure she has her brother or sister's attention. A child who is not paying attention is not likely to follow directions. Her sibling should be looking at her or focused on the play materials when she gives the instruction.

Table 6-1 | Giving Effective Commands

1. "Put man in truck."
2. "Throw me ball."
3. "Make cow say moo."
4. "Push car to garage."
5. "Give me doll."
6. "Give doll bottle."
7. "Make cat sounds."
8. "Help move chair."
9. "Put hands on drum."
10. "Blow bubbles."

The instructions that are given to children with ASD should be clear and uncomplicated. Table 6-1 gives examples of good instructions that are clear and easy to follow for young children. Notice that the requests for a very young child with limited language leave out the "small" words like "the" or "her." For a child with more complex understanding of speech, the directions can be more complex, but for a very early learner you want to be sure the key actions are highlighted in your speech and not lost in a lot of unnecessary verbiage.

Instructions should also be given at a slow enough pace for the child with an ASD to respond. The sibling-teacher should learn that it is important for him not to repeat himself, giving the same instruction again and again when his sister does not comply. He should ask his sister to do something (e.g.," Put doll on chair") and if she does not respond within five seconds, he should give her a verbal or physical prompt to do so. (See the section below on "Giving Help.") He should not keep repeating the command. This kind of "nagging" just teaches the child with an ASD that there is no hurry to comply as the instruction will be given multiple times. Without intending to, the person who repeats an instruction numerous times may be teaching a child to not comply with his instructions. Instead, if your child asks his sister to say the sound the dog makes and his sister does not comply, he could prompt her by softly saying "Woof" and then praising her if she imitates him.

Avoid vague or complicated, multiple commands such as "Stand up, put it over there, then get another one and bring it me and sit back down." A better way to give those same instructions would be to use proper nouns and break the instruction into several units. For example,

say 1) stand up, 2) put the car on the chair, 3) get another car, 4) bring the car to me, and 5) sit down by me. Your neurotypical child should give each of these commands one at a time and allow the sibling with an ASD five seconds to comply with each instruction. The simple and specific language, the slow pacing, and giving each of those instructions as a separate command increases the probability that his sister will be able to follow the whole sequence, one step at a time. For a child with more receptive language and a better memory, steps can be combined. For example, "Walk to the chair and get the blue car." Once that has been completed, "Now bring the car back and sit next to me."

If you child is having trouble learning how to give effective commands, spend some time with him playing the game of "Tell me what to do." In this game, which is a variation of "Simon Says," first you give him an instruction and then he gives you one. To make it fun you should give each other clear but sometimes silly directions, like "Put the bowl on your head like a hat," or, "Put your sock on your hand and your glove on your foot." As you play, give him feedback on his instructions, praising him for giving clear and specific directions. "Great job, you told me right where to put the car." Corrective feedback is also helpful. For example, "You told me to put it on the chair, but I wasn't sure what you meant by 'it.' Be sure to tell me the name of the object. For example, I would have said, 'Put bowl on chair.'"

Being Rewarding

Another essential of being a good teacher is providing enthusiastic praise and affection to the learner. Kids can do a terrific job at this! In teaching your son to play with his sister who is on the spectrum, your son must learn to reward good play behavior with specific praise. Saying such things as "Wow, that was great throwing the ball to me.

Way to go!" or "You found the yellow sticker! Gimme five!" This verbal praise should be spoken with energy and enthusiasm as well as specifying exactly what the child did right.

If necessary, your child can pair his praise of his sibling with small treats such as pieces of cookie or pretzel. But remember, the goal is for the play itself to become rewarding, so don't use edibles unless they are essential for getting started. If so, gradually fade them out as the children become more engaged in mutual play. Instead of food, your son could use a pat on the back, or a "high five" to reward his sister. Teach your child to deliver praise or other rewards immediately after his sibling does what has been requested. If he does need to use food in the beginning, tell him to always verbally praise his sister when he gives her a bit of food. When he pairs his praise with a bit of food, it is likely that his praise will become valued by her.

After the children have played for ten minutes or so you can provide a very natural food reward in the form of a desirable snack for both children. Cookies and milk or crackers and juice might be good. If your children enjoy other snacks like carrots or apple slices those would be fine. Whatever fits into their diets and pleases them is appropriate. This is a reward for both children. As they learn to play for longer intervals you can delay the snack until they are finished playing.

Another useful activity you can do with your son is to make up a long list of things he can say to praise his sister when she follows his instructions (Celiberti, 1993). This should be done at a separate time from the play sessions. See Table 6-2 for some examples of rewarding statements. Help you child think of statements he can

Table 6-2 | Being Rewarding

1. "Great job throwing ball."
2. "I like how you feed the doll."
3. "Great moo!"
4. "Wow, big bubbles!"
5. "You sound like a puppy. Good work!"
6. "What a big tower. Great building!"
7. "Nice throw, Tom."
8. "Good talking. You sound like the pilot."
9. "I have fun when we play trucks."
10. "Thanks for the doll. You're a terrific sister!"

make to his sister and don't forget to praise your son for his creative generation of new praise statements. Also, let him know once again how much you appreciate all the work he is doing to teach is sister how to play with him.

Another fun way to teach your child to be rewarding is for the two of you to play a game and allow him to play the role of teacher as he does with his sibling. Let him reinforce (reward) you with a penny each time you make a correct response, and you in turn should give him a penny for every effective praise statement he makes to you. He gets to keep all the pennies he earns. Older children may not need these games because they can learn simply by watching you and getting feedback from you. However, these games can be very helpful for allowing younger children to master the skills they need.

Giving Help

When a child with an ASD does not understand how to do a task, we can give her verbal or physical assistance (technically called a prompt) to follow the direction. For example, if your son wants to teach his sister to put a toy cow in the barn, he might say her name and then say, "Put cow in barn." He would give her five seconds to follow his instruction and if she did not respond he would take her hand, put it on the cow, and "walk" the cow into the barn with her, saying "Great job. You put cow in barn." Putting his hand over hers to enact walking the cow to the barn is an example of a full physical prompt.

It is very important that a child with ASD not become dependent on other people's physical prompts, so we always make sure to give the child time to respond on her own (up to five seconds for some children, less for children who are usually quicker to comply) and then we provide no more prompting than is essential. Gradually, we fade the prompt until it is no longer required. For example, if your son is teaching his sister to put the toy cow in the barn, he might make the touch of his physical prompt softer each time he makes the request, then try pointing to the cow (technically called a gestural prompt), and finally fade the prompt entirely. He should also make sure he gives his sister enough time to initiate the behavior on her own. But, if his sister starts to make a mistake, for example, if she is about to put the cow back into the box, he should not wait at all to prompt her, but immediately give her the physical guidance she needs to put the cow in the barn.

Prompting is the hardest to learn of the skills we have described. You should practice it with your child until he understands when to prompt and how to lessen his prompts. You can do this with a combination of modeling by you and feedback to your child as he practices first in a rehearsal with you and then in a play session with his sibling. We teach children to check the number of seconds they are waiting by saying to themselves, "count 1, count 2, count 3, count 4, count 5" as they count out the necessary number of seconds to wait until they offer the physical prompts.

If your child with an ASD does not like to be touched, her sibling should not be expected to use physical prompts until she has learned to tolerate them. Your first step should be to teach your child with ASD to accept this kind of contact from you, and then introduce the sibling's touch. Your child's teacher, the school psychologist, a physical therapist, or a Board Certified Behavior Analyst may have suggestions about how to increase your child's tolerance of touch.

Finishing Touches

There is one more valuable skill you can teach your neurotypical child to use in her interactions with her sibling with ASD. After your child has learned how to give instructions, to reward good behavior, and to provide physical or verbal guidance when necessary, she also needs to remember to reward spontaneous play behavior when your child with ASD initiates an interaction with her.

So far in this chapter we have focused on teaching a child with an ASD to follow instructions. However, play will be much more fun for both children when that child initiates the play! Your neurotypical child should be alert for those moments when they occur and reward them with as much enthusiasm and energy as possible. If your son has taught his sister to play catch with a big round ball and one day she picks up his football and throws it to him, he should express his pure delight. Similarly, if they have been playing with barnyard animals and she picks up a toy airplane, he should respond with a lot of energy to her initiation of a new game. The same should hold true for using new words. If she picks up the airplane and says "airplay," he can respond with "Yes, it is an airplane! Let's pretend to fly the airplane over the barn. I'll show you and then it will be your turn."

None of this is to say that your neurotypical child is obligated to stop whatever he is doing and always play with his sibling when she initiates it. Ideally, he should respond with warmth when he tells her he can't play at that moment. He can decline to play with her when he wants to play alone, study, or be with his friends. One of your roles as a parent is to help your child with an ASD accept these appropriate limits. For some children, a photographic activity schedule might be helpful in tolerating the delay. For example, there might be a sequence in which one picture might show her watching a DVD by herself, then eating dinner with the family, and then a third picture of her playing with her brother (McClannahan & Krantz, 2010).

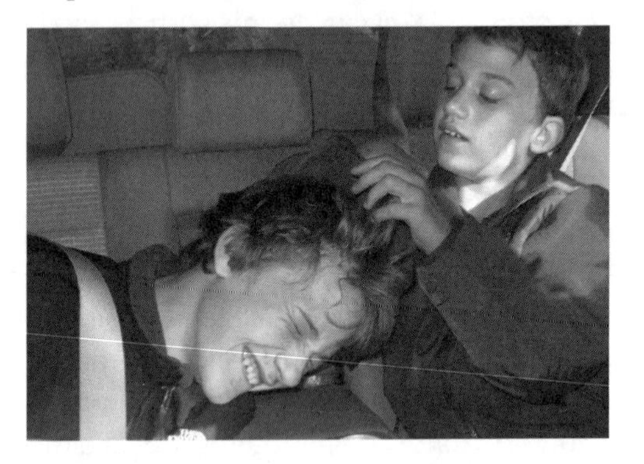

With Very Young Children

If your neurotypical child is younger than seven years old she may not be ready to assume the role of "teacher." For preschool- or kindergarten-aged children, a better approach is to play games that include both children and at least one parent. Sharing fun time together may help both children enjoy being with one another. For example, the "Come Here" game can be a big hit with young children. This involves calling the name of each child in turn and saying "Allison, come here," then being swept up into the adult's arms for a tickle, toss in the air, etc. Then it would be Tom's turn and he would be told to "come here" and then rewarded with some physical fun. In the beginning, it may be necessary to give the instruction from just a few feet away and for another adult or an older child to gently propel the child with an ASD to the adult who called her. Gradually, the distance can be increased and parents may call from different rooms of the house, while partially hidden, and so forth. Your typically developing preschooler will enjoy this game as will your young child with an ASD. The child learns that when you ask her to "come here," it is fun to comply. This compliance can be helpful when you want her to come from another room in the house or when she is outside and wandering toward the street.

Another similar game for preschool-aged children is a version of "Simon Says." It is the "Do This" game in which nonverbal imitation is rewarded in both children with hugs and applause. Again, your neurotypical child will like this as a game and your child with ASD is learning to imitate the gestures and actions of other people. As they get older and can understand the game of "Simon Says," the "Do This" game can gradually be expanded into that classic childhood game.

With Teens and Pre-Teens

Older children may want to teach their sibling with ASD additional skills beyond the simple play skills that have been our focus in this chapter. That can be wonderful for the entire family. But again, we feel strongly that they should not be forced into the role of teacher if they would rather do other things with their time.

If your child with ASD is on the higher end of the autism spectrum and able to play board games, competitive video games, sports, jogging, activities like shooting baskets or mini golf, both of your older children can enjoy these activities together. If your child on the spectrum has an intellectual disability as well as being on the autism spectrum, the activities with her sibling can become more age appropriate as they both grow up. For example, they might enjoy arts and crafts projects such as modeling with clay, painting and drawing, or perhaps building simple models of cars or planes. Many youngsters at any point on the spectrum may enjoy jogging with a sibling or parent. Training for that should start with very brief episodes and gradually increase in duration as both teens develop greater strength and endurance. That kind of vigorous activity can also be valuable in helping your teen with an ASD avoid the weight gain that occurs in many adolescents and adults on the spectrum who fail to be sufficiently active.

Your preteen or teenager may also be proud to be a tutor for a sibling on the spectrum. That might include academic skills, but we also know many teenagers who take pride in teaching their sibling on the spectrum meaningful life skills. For example, we know several teenage girls who taught their siblings how to match clothing so that their outfits were color and pattern coordinated. A teenaged boy we know took a lot of pride in teaching his brother on the spectrum how to shoot baskets. In all of these families, the initiation came from the teen—not the parents.

Closing Comments

Playing together is one of things that many children enjoy with their brother or sister. Perhaps you have fond memories of riding on the handlebars of your brother's bike, zooming down a hill on a sled with your sister, or some other activity that was fun for both of you. These shared activities help to build a positive sibling bond. When one child has an autism spectrum disorder, joint play is often disrupted by the seeming indifference of the child on the spectrum or by her difficult-to-manage behaviors. Fortunately, there is good research suggesting that neurotypical siblings can teach their brother or sister on the spectrum how to engage in play that becomes fun for both children. We outlined in this chapter how a typically developing child can learn to give instructions, provide rewards for appropriate play, and offer physical or verbal prompts to support the child with an ASD in learning play skills. Parents who understand the basics of applied behavior analysis can teach these skills to their neurotypical child and facilitate the development of a positive relationship between their children. It is also important, however, that parents be attuned to the wishes of the neurotypical child and not impose this learning as a duty, but rather offer it to the child who wishes to learn it.

Parents Speak

Over the years, some of the strategies I have used to develop the relationship between Matt, who has autism, and his sister Annie have revolved around play. Activities that involve music and song have been particularly effective—for example, "Row Row Row Your Boat," "Ring around the Rosie," "If You're Happy and You Know it," and "Wheels on the Bus." I have also taught Matt and Annie how to dance together.

Matt has always loved playing chase games, especially being surprised. I took it a step further, and taught them how to play "Hide and Seek." Matt has also learned how to direct Annie in a chase game through different rooms in the house. He chooses the path she'll take to run and surprise him (i.e., "Annie come chase me. Go through the living room"). In addition, I used the idea of chase for pretend play as well, for example, "playing monster."

Finally, my children have benefited from some more sedentary activities, such as coloring, playing with Play Doh, and reading. When the children were younger, I naturally did the reading. Now that Annie is learning to read, she loves to read to Matt and he is encouraged to do the same.

❧

My daughter learned how to go about getting eye contact and the value of reinforcement. The important thing about the play program is that it was designed for her and other siblings. She now has the basic skills necessary to successfully have fun with her brother. These skills could be carried over to all settings. My daughter is now important to her brother's life—she can help him, play with him, and laugh with him. What a boost to her self-esteem and family harmony.

❧

When you sent home a letter to my mom asking her about siblings, I asked her if I could write to you. She said sure, so here it is. I want you to know how great it is to play with Art. Sometimes I still get mad at him. But I like it when he learns to throw the ball with me and roll cars. Next, I'm going to teach him to pretend to be an animal like a dog or cat or lion.

❧

When I first started to get my kids to play together, I wondered if it was more work than it was worth. Eric, my boy with autism, can be a tough cookie, and he could really give my daughter, Sarah, a hard time. For a long time, I pretty much had to sit there and watch so I could pick Eric up and put him in time out if he got rowdy. But, gradually he started to enjoy being with Sarah, and now it is rare that he gets out of control. When he does, Sarah knows to call me and I put him in time out. It took three or four months to get it rolling, but now it works pretty well.

❧

Maurice and Ada play together in their own nonsensical way and have a unique bond. He knows she isn't a parent, but a full-time playmate, friend, and sometimes nuisance! She knows how much he can take and that if she crosses that line will receive a scream from him, or worse, an aggression. In turn, he also knows the boundaries with her.

7 All Grown Up
The Mature Sibling

The Levine Family

Hannah began her career as a special education lawyer at a very young age. Eight years old to be exact. She has clear memories of sitting in on IEP meetings for her brother, Samuel, and jumping into the conversation to correct the adults about what actually would work best for him. She recalls reminding her parents of requests that they had intended to raise and forgotten, and as she got older, correcting the child study team members about what Samuel was, in fact, entitled to.

Sadly, at that time, options for intervention were far more limited than they are today, especially around challenging behaviors. She remembers being taught by her brother's teachers how to spray Samuel with an ammonia solution if he became aggressive, and watching him be physically restrained by multiple adults. But, she also has a lot of fond memories of watching her brother's favorite TV shows with him, or watching Samuel wordlessly flirt with attractive instructors at his group home.

All of that experience with perceived injustice, and striving for justice, for someone she loves, doubtlessly shaped Hannah's life and career choice. Today, at thirty-five years old, she is still fighting for the rights of children with disabilities, just as she fought for Samuel at those early IEP meetings.

Samuel now lives in a group home where Hannah shares the responsibility with her parents of visiting him and keeping an eye on things. She takes Samuel out to see live performances of his favorite shows, and introduces him to all of her potential boyfriends. She has chosen to play a very active role in her brother's life.

In contrast, Hannah's younger brother, Joshua, has chosen a different path. Joshua is an architect with a thriving business. He married at a young age and has three kids of his own. Joshua sees Samuel at family gatherings, and has agreed to help pay for services Samuel may need in the future. Joshua is happy to lend an ear when his parents or his sister need to talk about Samuel, and is listed as the next person to call in an emergency after his parents and Hannah. However, Joshua prefers a more separate life for himself.

Introduction

We are often asked by parents, "What happens to siblings of children with ASD when they grow up? How do they turn out?" Unfortunately, that is an impossible question to answer. Each sibling of a child with ASD will follow a different path. You might as well ask, "What happens to children when they grow up?" No one answer will do the trick. Even within the same family, siblings will often grow up with very little personality-resemblance to one another. The same holds true for siblings of children with ASD. Each will follow his own path, and what that path will look like is anyone's guess.

Families like the Levine's are not atypical. It is very common in families with multiple typically developing children for siblings to have widely varying degrees of involvement with the individual with

ASD. Some adult children seem to define themselves in terms of the experience of being raised with a sibling on the spectrum. It shapes their career choice, family planning, social activities, etc. Other siblings have completely separate interests.

One of us (BG) moderated a panel of adult siblings of individuals on the spectrum for a conference. The panelists varied greatly in their degree of involvement with the world of ASD. One panelist was a computer technologist who went away from home to college, and settled down near his college town. He loved his brother on the spectrum and visited him periodically, but left the caretaking responsibilities to his parents. Another panelist was a special education teacher who specialized in working with children with ASD, and visited her brother with ASD often, as well as corresponded with him frequently via email. A third panelist provides an example of someone who chose the middle ground. As a beauty pageant contestant, autism had been her platform, and she has been active in raising both funds and awareness. However, her passion was engineering and she was actively pursuing an engineering degree and career. These panelists exemplify the spectrum of choices that might be made by siblings.

Changing Times

Today's adults, like Hannah and Joshua, have experienced a very different world than the adult siblings of tomorrow will. Today, with the advent of inclusive education practices, more and more children with disabilities are attending public schools, which means more and more siblings are sharing the bus stop, the cafeteria, and the hallways with their brothers or sisters on the spectrum. Does this make siblings more comfortable because their classmates are more familiar with autism? Or does this make siblings less comfortable because more peers know about their brother's or sister's challenges? More effective interventions mean that there are more mildly affected children with ASD than there were in the past. Does this strengthen sibling bonds as individuals on the spectrum grow more responsive? Or does this further challenge relationships, as behavioral difficulties become less and less obviously related to disability? These are questions with no known answers at this time.

Similarly, Hannah and Joshua's experiences look nothing like the experiences of siblings from previous generations. A sixty-year-old adult sibling living today probably had a sibling with ASD who was institutionalized. The message then was that not much could be done to improve either the child's or the family's quality of life if they kept their child at home. How does this shape his role as an adult sibling? These adults were likely raised in homes that did not support inclusion, nor did many families at that time receive training as to how to most successfully interact with individuals on the spectrum. The fact that there used to be no hope of improvement offered to families of children with autism would have had a significant impact on a sibling's experience. This may affect one's willingness to visit or bring home a sibling with ASD even to this day.

In summary, changing trends in society's response to ASD and the efficacy of existing treatments prevent us from being able to predict much about one generation of adult siblings based on what we know about another. However, one thing we do know about adult siblings across the generations is that they will have many of the same choices to face as their forerunners.

Choices

As children, our parents orchestrate many of our interactions with our siblings. For example, they may structure the activities siblings share and ensure that each child also pursues independent activities. They may also determine how much time the family will spend together. When we reach adulthood, the sibling relationship is typically self-defined. It is the siblings who determine how often to call one another, how often to visit, and how much of their lives to share. These same decisions hold true for siblings of individuals with ASD. While parents may hope for a certain quality of relationship between their children, the ultimate decision falls to the siblings. Furthermore, many adults with ASD may not be able to pick up a phone or hop in the car for a visit. As a result, it often ends up being the neurotypical sibling who chooses the frequency of interaction.

As with any sets of siblings, some adult siblings of individuals with ASD pursue a close relationship with their affected brother or sister. And some do not. In our experience, we have come across siblings with a wide range of approaches to their relationships. Some young adults exercise their new-found independence by creating a life that is free from what they perceive to be the burdens associated with their sibling. Others describe strong feelings of love and attachment to siblings and wish to remain a part of their lives. Still others may feel responsible for their siblings and assume a care-giving role. Whichever choice an adult sibling makes is a legitimate one.

We have found that there is not one typical outcome for adult relationships with people with ASD. Furthermore, feelings and perspectives change over time. Because a relationship has one form today does not guarantee that it will not have a different form tomorrow.

When one has a brother or sister with autism, the relationship decisions may take on much higher stakes than usual. Many individuals with ASD will need assistance as adults and some individuals with ASD will not be able to live independently. An adult sibling may ultimately be responsible for ensuring a safe and high quality residence for his brother or sister on the spectrum. This may be in the form of a group home, supervised apartment, or even semi-independent living with oversight. A sibling may have to decide how to manage the cost and day-to-day responsibilities incurred by these varying arrangements.

Whatever form of residence is decided upon for an adult with ASD, a sibling will have to decide how this will affect his living situation. What if he is offered a terrific job opportunity across the country? What if the best college for his major is a fifteen hour drive from his sister? What if a sibling becomes involved in a long distance romance? The sibling will have to choose how to balance caretaking with pursuing his own goals and dreams.

More broadly speaking, as adults, siblings will determine how much of their identity to ascribe to growing up with a brother or sister with ASD. Many adult siblings have told us that potential spouses have to be well acquainted with the brother or sister with ASD and "pass the test" of interacting well with him or her. As most adults with neurotypical siblings wouldn't think of requiring sibling approval of a suitor, this suggests that the sibling with ASD has emerged as a large part of who these neurotypical adult siblings have become.

Furthermore, there has been speculation that adult siblings of individuals with disabilities are more likely to work in helping professions, although the evidence on this is mixed. Siblings that go into fields such as special education, medicine, psychology, and speech therapy may have done so anyway, or it may be that their experiences growing up with a brother or sister with special needs has helped shape who they are. Many siblings will choose to go into a variety of careers based on their own interests, unrelated to special needs. Any vocational choice can be healthy if it is freely made.

Adult siblings are faced with a multitude of choices in relation to their brother or sister with ASD. Some of the choices will align with parental hopes and dreams. Other choices will disappoint parents. Although it may be painful for parents, it is important that they accept their child's right to make these decisions. Siblings may feel very resentful if their parents try to dictate how much they should include the individual with ASD in their world. This can then act as a wedge between the siblings. Conversely, accepting a typically developing child's feelings and giving him full permission to experience those feelings is likely to promote a healthier sibling relationship.

This does not mean that parents must condone all decisions made by their typically developing child about his sibling, but disagreements should be couched in terms that make it clear that parents respect their adult child's authority to define his own relationships. For example, a parent might say, "I understand how you feel about

Tim. It can be hard to include him in your life—it requires you to make a lot of sacrifices. I see that. But, I know that his successes have brought you a lot of joy as well, and that your visits really do make a big difference to him. For the sake of both of you, I hope that one day you'll decide that you'd like him back in your life." In the event that a sibling's choices and a parent's preferences do not match, and these conflicts cannot be resolved harmoniously, it can often be helpful to participate in family counseling.

Even after incorporating the suggestions above, a parent may find that his typically developing child wants very little to do with his brother or sister with autism. This is not a parent's fault and does not signify a failure on the part of the parent. Many variables affect a sibling's decisions regarding his brother or sister with ASD. Among other factors, children grow up contending with the influence of peers, the severity of their sibling's disability, and varying degrees of resources available to the family. Parents cannot claim sole responsibility for the quality of their children's adult relationships. With that said, it is worthwhile to note that in our experience, it is far more common for siblings to maintain loving, devoted relationships than it is for them to lose touch with one another. The vast majority of adult siblings that we meet are constantly seeking information about how to be more supportive of their brother or sister rather than seeking separate lives. Parents should keep this in mind when they worry how their children will relate to one another in the future.

Some parents will experience the challenge of an adult sibling becoming so involved with their sibling on the spectrum that it is unclear who has the final say when decisions need to be made. Adult siblings may become educated and active caregivers, and it might be hard for a parent to justify keeping sole rights to the final say. Keeping an open mind to a collaborative approach will probably lead to the best results for everyone involved. Joint discussions with active listening will be enormously helpful in understanding everyone's point of view and reaching an optimal decision. If differences still cannot be resolved, consider seeking the advice of a neutral third party. Someone from a national or local autism agency may be able to share what they've learned from their experience. Similarly, a professional (e.g., psychologist, social worker) who has been helpful to the individual with ASD and knows him well may be able to offer some guidance.

Financial and Legal Considerations

Although Hannah, from the earlier case study, is an extreme example, many children participate in advocacy from an early age. If parents see that their typically developing child appears interested in assuming the role of advocate and caregiver for their sibling, they should be sure to pass on the benefits of their experience as much as possible. It is best to start sharing relevant information while the neurotypical child is living at home. This can be done without placing any expectation on the child about what his role will be in relation to his sibling as an adult. Often, these children are fluent advocates by the time their skills are needed. They will grow up understanding their sibling's rights.

Ideally, parents and siblings should discuss what is involved in assuming caretaking responsibility long before it becomes necessary. Topics to discuss include:

1. *How have the financial needs of the individual with ASD been met since he became an adult?* How will the financial plan change after the parents' death? How much money, if any, will the siblings need to contribute to meet his needs? Are there changes that the parents or siblings could make to their wills or life insurance policies to better provide for the individual with autism, as well as other family members?
2. *What needs does the individual with autism have for a guardian at present and how might those needs change over time?* If the parents have been acting as guardian, is the sibling automatically the best choice to take over as guardian? If not, the parents and the sibling can

work jointly to identify a better choice. If the individual with ASD already has a guardian, what does that person do for him?

3. *What benefits has the person with ASD been receiving from the federal government or other sources?* Medical care? Housing assistance? Vocational rehabilitation? Social Security? What does the sibling need to know about preserving those benefits?

In discussing these issues, parents and siblings would probably be wise to consult a lawyer who has experience in the disabilities arena. Regulations can be complex, and an experienced lawyer can navigate these regulations and prevent cessation of benefits, pilfering of trusts, and other concerns. An attorney can also assist a sibling in gaining the legal power to make medical decisions for his sibling, or to decide where a sibling will live. These types of decisions require a legal appointment.

Finally, adults with disabilities have special rights with regard to employment, housing, healthcare, and other areas. In order to be an effective advocate for a brother or sister, a sibling needs to become well versed with laws pertaining to individuals with disabilities. National agencies such as The Autism Society (of America), and state agencies such as your state Protection & Advocacy agency (see Resource Guide) can be helpful in obtaining updated, easy-to-read summaries of advocacy information. There may also be state autism agencies or organizations that can help point you in the right direction.

Marriage and Family

As noted above, many potential spouses of siblings with ASD must "pass the test" before being considered. Siblings have shared that there are two reasons for "the test." The first is an attitude of "My sibling with ASD is a part of me—love me, love my sibling." The second thought often articulated to us is that siblings often worry about having children with ASD of their own. In the event that their child is, in fact, born with an ASD, they want to ensure that the potential partner will not shy away from their own child should he have a disability. One sibling went so far as to describe her brother with ASD as the perfect test.

She explained that you can tell the most about a person's character by how they treat people with less power. Because of her brother's developmental problems, she felt that he was usually the person with the least power in the interaction, and watching people with him revealed their true character.

Additionally, some siblings feel that having potential spouses spend time with their brother or sister with ASD is appropriate because it prepares them for what family gatherings will be like, and creates an opportunity to discuss potential caregiving possibilities. These siblings are trying to offer full disclosure before a commitment is made.

Being an adult sibling of an individual with ASD may also influence childbearing choices. Adult siblings face tough questions regarding their possible genetic makeup. Although the specific causes of ASD are not known, what is known is that for many people with ASD, there is a genetic component (Folstein & Rosen-Sheidley, 2001). Unless he is an identical twin, there is a low probability that a sibling of an individual with ASD will himself have a child with ASD. Nevertheless, sharing the genetic heritage of an individual with ASD does increase the risk of having a child with this disability compared to other adults. Especially as the prevalence of ASD continues to climb, the increased risk might be especially scary to a sibling as he might truly understand the myriad ways that a family member with ASD changes one's life.

In contrast, some siblings of individuals with ASD report feeling empowered as they contemplate the parenting role. For better or worse, these siblings are experienced caregivers by the time they reach child bearing age. Additionally, many of today's siblings of individuals with ASD are well trained in various aspects of behavior management and skill development. Again, these skills help siblings feel more prepared for parenting roles.

Although rare, some siblings of individuals with ASD assume caregiving roles for the children of their brothers or sisters with ASD.

Sex education and family planning are important and challenging issues in all families, but they take on added complexity for individuals with ASD. As a result, contraception is not always explained or provided to individuals on the spectrum, who may not understand enough about sex to know that pregnancy may result. Because these individuals may lack the skills to care even for themselves, the baby might be raised by an adult sibling.

Resources for Adult Siblings

While child siblings of today may meet other siblings of children with ASD through their brother's school or a local sibling discussion group, these options are rarely available for adult siblings. Especially if a sibling is geographically separated from his brother and his service providers, he may be disconnected from the autism community. This can lead to feelings of isolation for the adult sibling.

One source of information and connection that may meet the needs of adult siblings is SibNet, a collaboration between the Sibling Support Project and the Sibling Leadership Network. This group offers online information and support to siblings of individuals with ASD of all ages. General information about sibling issues can be found at their website: http://www.siblingsupport.org/connect/the-sibnet-listserv. Furthermore, through their Facebook page and Yahoogroup, SibNet offers connections specific to adult siblings of individuals with ASD's. As many adult siblings will tell you, this type of information, and support from others who have been there, can be invaluable. SibNet also offers information about events for adult siblings that take place across the nation.

Local agencies that serve individuals with ASD and related disabilities may also have information relevant to adult siblings. For example, in South Carolina, the Division of Disabilities Council runs an adult sibling leadership network offering information on the state's system of supports and services as well as social connection. Check your local office of disabilities or ASD advocacy group to find out if there is a forum for adult siblings in your region.

Counseling services from a psychologist or other therapist familiar with ASD can provide another helpful resource for siblings. Through counseling, a sibling might explore the impact of his brother's or sister's disability on his life path and the decisions that he has made, or the influence of experiences with his sibling on choices that he needs to make in the future. Some siblings may first fully realize in adulthood that their experiences as a brother or sister were not the same as those of their peers. This realization may trigger feelings of loss, disappointment, or even anger. Working through these emotions with a competent therapist can be extremely helpful. Other siblings may need support around feelings related to the relationship that they have created with their brother or sister. For example, assuming caretaking responsibilities may be overwhelming at first and involves a shift in one's sense of identity.

It is important for siblings to remember that participation in counseling does not imply that one has a "problem," but it does go a long way in helping people feel good about themselves and preventing the onset of any serious problems. For referrals to local counselors with relevant expertise, contact local autism agencies.

Closing Comments

Adult siblings of individuals with ASD make a tremendous number of choices in relation to their brother or sister on the spectrum. When siblings grow up with an understanding of ASD, and helpful behavioral, emotional, financial, and legal strategies, they can act as confident adults ready to tackle the tough decisions in front of them. The challenges of adulthood, while still demanding, will loom far less daunting than they would to an unarmed sibling. By generously sharing support and information, parents are preparing their typically developing children for a far less stressful experience as an adult sibling of an individual on the spectrum.

Parents and Siblings Speak

I worry about when they are both teenagers and my daughter will want more privacy. I don't think my son will understand concepts like nudity, good manners, personal space, etc. She may become distant from him. I hope I'll be understanding of this and realize that in the future they will become close again.

My husband and I do not want the burden of taking care of our son to fall on our daughter. We hope she will be able to live her life as if her brother were "neurotypical." As she gets older, we worry about her future and have concerns (should she want to start a family) about the genetic aspect of the disorder.

When I was a kid, it seemed to me that my brother Rich, who has autism, got the lion's share of attention in our house. Now that I am an adult, I can understand the jam my parents were in, but it was tough for me when I was younger. I love Rich, and my wife and I invite him to spend holidays with us, but I try to make sure my own kids understand why Uncle Rich needs so much of Dad's time when he visits.

I guess it isn't an accident that I ended up as a pediatrician. All the time I was growing up, I kept praying there would by a way to cure Rich.

I will always be grateful to my parents for how they talked to me when I was kid. They told me about my brother's autism, and they seemed to be able to understand when I teased him or pushed him around a little. I mean they didn't say it was OK, but they didn't do a real guilt trip either. They would punish me the same way my best friend got punished when he would tease his little sister. No more and no less. Plus, they would help me find things I could do that would give me a way to play with my brother. It wasn't ideal, and I think they made mistakes like all parents do, but I always knew they would listen to me and try to be fair. I appreciate that all the more now that I'm grown and know how hard it must have been on them raising the two of us and him having autism.

References

Anderson, S.R., Jablonski, A.L., Thomeer, M.L., & Knapp, V.M. (2007). *Self-help skills for people with autism: A systematic teaching approach*. Bethesda, MD: Woodbine House.

Bank, S.P. & Kahn, M.D. (1982). *The sibling bond*. NY: Basic Books.

Bibace, R. & Walsh, M.E. (1979). Developmental stages in children's conceptions of illness. In G.C. Stone & N.E. Adler (Eds.), *Health Psychology* (pp. 285-301). San Francisco: Jossey Bass.

Bibace, R. & Walsh, M.E. (1980). Development of children's concepts of illness. *Pediatrics, 66,* 912-917.

Boer, F., Goehardt, A.W., & Treffers, P.D.A. (1992). Siblings and their parents. In F. Boer & J. Dunn (Eds.), *Children's sibling relationships: Developmental and clinical issues* (pp. 41-54). Hillsdale, NJ: Erlbaum Associates.

Bondy, A. & Frost, L. (2011). *A picture's worth: PECS and other visual communication strategies in autism*. 2nd Ed. Bethesda, MD: Woodbine House.

Brodzinsky, D.M., Singer, L., & Braff, A.M. (1984). Children's understanding of adoption. *Child Development, 55,* 869-878.

Buggey, T. (2009). Seeing is believing: Video self-modeling for people with autism and other developmental disabilities. Bethesda, MD: Woodbine House.

Buhrmester, D. (1992). The developmental course of sibling and peer relationships. In F. Boer & J. Dunn (Eds.), *Children's sibling relationships: Developmental and clinical issues* (pp. 1-40). Hillsdale, NJ: Erlbaum Associates.

Campbell, J.M. & Barger, B.D. (2011). Middle school students' knowledge of autism. *Journal of Autism and Developmental Disorders, 41, 6,* 732-740.

Carandang, M.L.A., Folkins, C.H., Hines, P.A., & Steward, M.S. (1979). The role of cognitive level and sibling illness in children's conceptualizations of illness. *American Journal of Orthopsychiatry, 49,* 474-481.

Celiberti, D.A. (1993). *Training parents of children with autism to promote sibling play: Randomized trials of three alternative training interventions*. Unpublished doctoral dissertation, Rutgers, the State University of New Jersey, Piscataway, NJ.

Celiberti, D.A. & Harris, S.L. (1993). The effects of a play skills intervention for siblings of children with autism. *Behavior Therapy, 24,* 573-599.

Cicirelli, V.G. (1995). *Sibling relationships across the life span.* New York: Plenum Press.

Dunn, J. (1992). Sisters and brothers: Current issues in developmental research. In F. Boer & J. Dunn (Eds.), *Children's sibling relationships: Developmental and clinical issues* (pp. 1-40). Hillsdale, NJ: Erlbaum Associates.

El-Ghoroury, N.H. & Romanczyk, R.G. (1999). Play interactions of family members towards children with autism. *Journal of Autism and Developmental Disorders, 29,* 249-258.

Ferraioli, S.J. & Harris, S.L. (2011). Teaching joint attention to children with autism through sibling-mediated behavioral intervention. *Behavioral Interventions, 26,* 261-281.

Folstein, S.E. & Rosen-Sheidley, B., (2001) Genetics of autism: Complex aetiology for a heterogeneous disorder. *Nature Reviews, 2,* 943-955.

Forgatch, M. & Patterson, G. (1989). *Parents and adolescents living together, Part 2: Family Problem solving.* Eugene, OR: Castalia Publishing Co.

Gamliel, I., Yirmiya, N., & Sigman, M. (2007). The development of young siblings of children with autism from 4 to 54 months. *Journal of Autism and Developmental Disorders, 37,* 171-183.

Glasberg, B.A. (2000). The development of siblings' understanding of autism and related disorders. *Journal of Autism and Developmental Disorders, 30 (2),* 143-156.

Grissom, O.M. & Borkowski, J.G. (2002). Self-efficacy in adolescents who have siblings with or without disabilities. *American Journal on Mental Retardation, 107,* 79-90.

Harris, S.L., Handleman, J.S., & Palmer, C. (1985). Parents and grandparents view the autistic child. *Journal of Autism and Developmental Disorders, 15,* 127-137.

Knighting, K., Rowa-Dewar, N., Malcolm, C., Kearney, N., & Gibson, F. (2011). Children's understanding of cancer and views on health-related behaviour: A "draw and write" study. *Child Care Health Development, 37(2),* 289-99.

Kurdek, L.A. (1986). Children's reasoning about parental divorce. In R.D. Ashmore & D.M. Brodzinsky, (Eds.) *Thinking about the family: Views of parents and children* (pp. 233-276). Hillsdale, NJ: Lawrence Erlbaum Associates.

Leaf, R. & McEachin, J. (1999) *A work in progress: Behavior management strategies and a curriculum for intensive behavioral treatment of autism.* New York: DRL Books, L.L.C.

Lobato, D. (1990). *Brothers, sisters and special needs.* Baltimore, MD: Paul H. Brookes.

Lovaas, O.I., Koegel, R., Simmons, J.Q., & Long, J.S. (1973). Some generalization and follow-up measures on autistic children in behavior therapy. *Journal of Applied Behavior Analysis, 6 (1),* 131-166.

McClanahan, L.E. & Krantz, P.J. (2010). *Activity schedules for children with autism: Teaching independent behavior.* 2nd Ed. Bethesda, MD: Woodbine House.

McHale, S.M., & Harris, V.S. (1992). Children's experiences with disabled and nondisabled siblings: Links with personal adjustment and relationship evaluations. In F. Boer & J. Dunn (Eds.), *Children's sibling relationships: Developmental and clinical issues* (pp. 83-100). Hillsdale, NJ: Erlbaum Associates.

McHale, S.M., Sloan, J., & Simeonsson, R.J. (1986). Sibling relationships of children with autistic, mentally retarded, and nonhandicapped brothers and sisters. *Journal of Autism and Developmental Disorders, 16,* 399-413.

Meyer, D.J. & Vadasy, P.F. (2008). *Sibshops: Workshops for siblings of children with special needs,* Revised Ed. Baltimore, MD: Paul H. Brookes.

Osborne, M.L., Kistner, J.A., & Helgemo, B. (1993). Developmental progression in children's knowledge of AIDS: Implications for education and attitudinal change. *Journal of Pediatric Psychology, 18,* 177-192.

Piaget, J. (1929). *The child's conception of the world.* New York: Harcourt Brace Jovanovich.

Poltorak, D.Y. & Glazer, J.P. (2006). The development of children's understanding of death: Cognitive and psychodynamic considerations. *Child & Adolescent Psychiatric Clinics of North America, 15 (3),* 567-573.

Rodrigue, J.R., Geffken, G.R., & Morgan, S.B. (1993). Perceived competence and behavioral adjustment of siblings of children with autism. *Journal of Autism and Developmental Disorders, 23,* 665-674.

Rozga, A., Hutman, T., Young, G.S., Rogers, S.J., Oznoff, S., Dapretto, M., & Sigman, M. (2011). Behavioral profiles of affected and unaffected siblings of children with autism: Contributions of measures of mother-infant interaction and nonverbal communication. *Journal of Autism and Developmental Disorders, 41*, 287-301.

Seligman, M. & Darling, R.B. (1977). *Ordinary families, special children*. 2nd Ed. New York: Guilford Press.

Slomkowski, C. & Manke, B. (2004). Sibling relationships during childhood: Multiple perceptions from multiple perspectives. In R.D. Conger, F.O. Lorenz, & K.A.S. Wickrama (Eds.), *Continuity and change in family relations: Theory, methods, and empirical findings* (pp. 293-317). Mahwah, NJ: Lawrence Erlbaum Associates.

Strohm, K. (2005). *Being the other one: Growing up with a brother or sister who has special needs.* Boston, MA: Shambhala Publications.

Toth, K., Dawson, G., Meltzoff, A.N., Greenson, J., & Fein, D. (2007). Early social, imitation, play, and language abilities of young non-autistic siblings of children with autism. *Journal of Autism and Developmental Disorders, 37*, 145-157.

Weiss, M.J. & Harris, S.L. (2001). *Reaching out, joining in: Teaching social skills to young children with autism.* Bethesda, MD: Woodbine House.

Resource Guide

Organizations and Resources for Siblings

The Arc
1825 K Street NW
Suite 1200
Washington, DC 20006
202-534-3700; 800-433-5255
www.thearc.org

A grassroots organization that works to include all children and adults with cognitive and developmental disabilities in every community. Provides information, online discussion group, and links to local services for siblings.

The Autism Society (of America)
4340 East-West Highway
Suite 350
Bethesda, MD 20814
800-328-8476
www.autism-society.org

A national organization of parents and professionals that promotes a better understanding of autism, encourages the development of services, supports autism related research, and advocates on behalf of people with autism and their families. Provides information and links to other supports for siblings.

Autism Society Canada
P.O. Box 22017
1670 Heron Road
Ottawa, Ontario
K1V 0C2
613-789-8943; 866-476-8440
www.autismsocietycanada.ca

A national nonprofit organization committed to advocacy, public education, information and referral, and advocacy. Has a wealth of resources and links specifically for siblings.

Autism New Jersey
500 Horizon Drive
Suite 530
Robbinsville, NJ 08691
609-588-8200; 800-4-AUTISM
www.autismnj.org

A nonprofit agency providing information and advocacy services, family and professional education, and consultation. Offers a sibling pen pal program for siblings of varied ages.

National Autistic Society
393 City Road
London, EC1V 1NG
United Kingdom
+44 (0)20-7833-2299
www.autism.org.uk

The UK's foremost organization for people with autism and those who care about them. Provides guidelines for siblings, real life stories, and links to useful websites.

Sibling Support Project
6512 23rd Ave NW, #213
Seattle, WA 98117
206-297-6368
www.siblingsupport.org

A national nonprofit organization devoted to siblings of individuals with disabilities. Sponsors listservs for siblings of different ages as well as parents. Also provides free access to information and publications.

"Siblings of Autistic Children" page on **Facebook**

An opportunity to connect online with other siblings of individuals with ASD.

Sibs

Meadowfield, Oxenhope, West Yorkshire, BD22 9JD
01535 645453
www.sibs.org.uk

A UK charity representing the needs of siblings of people with disabilities. Provides information and support to siblings and parents via email or phone.

U.S. Department of Health and Human Services
Administration for Children & Families
Administration on Developmental Disabilities
State Protection and Advocacy Agencies
370 L'Enfant Promenade, SW
Washington, DC 20447
http://www.acf.hhs.gov/programs/add/states/pas.html

Books about ASD and Special Needs for Siblings

Books for Young Children

Bishop, B. (2011). *My Friend with Autism: Enhanced Edition with FREE CD of Coloring Pages!* Arlington, TX: Future Horizons.

Edwards, B. & Armitage, D. (2012). *My Brother Sammy is Special.* New York, NY: Sky Pony Press.

Lears, L. (1998). *Ian's Walk: A Story about Autism*. Park Ridge, IL: Albert Whitman & Company.

Peete, H.R. & Peete, R.E. (2010). *My Brother Charlie*. New York, NY: Scholastic.

Thompson, M. (1996). *Andy and His Yellow Frisbee*. Bethesda, MD: Woodbine House.

van Niekerk, C. & Venter, L. (2008). *Understanding Sam and Asperger Syndrome*. Erie, PA: Skeezel Press.

Books for Older Children

Bristow, C. (2008). *My Strange and Terrible Malady.* Overland Park, KS: Autism Asperger Publishing Company.

Haddon, M. (2004). *The Curious Incident of the Dog in the Night-Time.* New York, NY: Knopf.

Jackson, L. (2002). *Freaks, Geeks & Asperger Syndrome: A User Guide to Adolescence.* London, England: Jessica Kingsley Publishers.

Keating-Velasco, J. (2007). *A Is for Autism, F Is for Friend: A Kid's Book for Making Friends with a Child Who Has Autism.* Overland Park, KS: Autism Asperger Publishing Company.

Lord, C. (2008) *Rules.* New York, NY: Scholastic.

Books about Being a Sibling

Feiges, L.S. & Weiss, M.J. (2004). *Sibling Stories: Reflections on Life with a Brother or Sister on the Autism Spectrum.* Overland Park, KS: Autism Asperger Publishing Company.

Meyer, D. (1997). *Views from Our Shoes: Growing Up with a Brother or Sister with Special Needs*. Bethesda, MD: Woodbine House.

Meyer, D. (2005). *The Sibling Slam Book: What It's Really Like to Have a Brother or Sister with Special Needs*. Bethesda, MD: Woodbine House.

Meyer, D., Ed. (2009) *Thicker Than Water: Essays by Adult Siblings of People with Disabilities.* Bethesda, MD: Woodbine House.

Meyer, D. & Vadasy, P. (1996). *Living with a Brother or Sister with Special Needs: A Book for Sibs.* Seattle, WA: University of Washington Press.

Shapiro, O. (2009). *Autism and Me: Sibling Stories*. Park Ridge, IL: Albert Whitman & Company.

Websites with Information on Typical Development

American Academy of Pediatrics
www.aap.org/healthtopics/stages.cfm

Centers for Disease Control and Prevention
www.cdc.gov/ncbddd/actearly/milestones/index.html

Public Broadcasting Service
www.pbs.org/wholechild/abc/index.html

If you have concerns about your neurotypical child's development:

For Babies and Toddlers:

Check out Autism Speaks' list of "Baby Sibs Consortium Researchers" with expertise in developmental problems commonly seen among siblings of individuals with ASD.
http://www.autismspeaks.org/science/initiatives/high-risk-baby-sibs/consortium-researchers

For Older Children:

Take your child to a developmental-behavioral pediatrician. To find a specialist near you, use the American Academy of Pediatrics website: http://www.healthychildren.org/english/family-life/health-management/pediatric-specialists/pages/what-is-a-developmental-behavioral-pediatrician.aspx

If you feel your child needs psychological support:

Use the locator service on the American Psychological Association website: http://locator.apa.org

Index

About the Authors

Sandra L. Harris, Ph.D. is a Board of Governors Distinguished Service Professor Emerita at the Graduate School of Applied and Professional Psychology and the Department of Psychology at Rutgers, the State University of New Jersey. She is the Founder and Executive Director of the Douglass Developmental Disabilities Center at Rutgers. The Center serves people with autism spectrum disorder from toddlers through adulthood. She was the Rutgers University recipient of the 2005 President's Award for Research in Service to New Jersey.

Beth A. Glasberg, Ph.D., BCBA-D is the Coordinator for the Masters Program in Applied Psychology, Behavior Analysis Concentration at Rider University in Lawrenceville, NJ. She is also the Director of Glasberg Behavioral Consulting Services, LLC, which supports individuals in their social, academic, and behavioral skill development. She is a Board Certified Behavior Analyst and two-time recipient of The Lebec Prize for Research in Autism.